THE POWER ✓ OF POSITIVE MANAGEMENT

Books by the same author

Positive Mind Power
Positive Mind Therapy
Think Positive and Things Will Go Right
21 Laws of Positive Living

THE POWER OF POSITIVE MANAGEMENT

A practical guide for professionals

Rakesh K Mittal

A Sterling Paperback

STERLING PAPERBACKS
An imprint of
Sterling Publishers (P) Ltd.
A-59, Okhla Industrial Area, Phase-II,
New Delhi-110020.
Tel: 26387070, 26386209; Fax: 91-11-26383788
E-mail: sterlingpublishers@airtelbroadband.in
ghai@nde.vsnl.net.in
www.sterlingpublishers.com

The Power of Positive Management
© 2006, Rakesh K Mittal
ISBN 81 207 3107 3

All rights are reserved.
No part of this publication may be reproduced, stored in a retrieval system or transmitted, in any form or by any means, mechanical, photocopying, recording or otherwise, without prior written permission of the original publisher.

Printed and Published by Sterling Publishers Pvt. Ltd., New Delhi-110 020.

Contents

Foreword	vii
Preface	ix
Our Dilemma	1
The Missing Dimension	4
The Human Element in Management	9
Positive Thinking for Excellence	16
Integrity	24
Plan Your Money	27
Plan Your Time	31
Motivate Your Subordinates	37
Plan Your Meetings	41
Dealing with Official Documents	45
Effective Touring	49
Appraising Subordinates	53
Efficient Use of the Telephone	56
Organising a Conference	63
Be Transparent	70
Meeting Visitors	76
Organise Your Court Work	81
Management of Legal Cases	83
Relations with Colleagues/Peer Group	87

Disposal of Files	92
Relations with Politicians	97
Making an Effective Speech	102
Relations with the Media	107
Managing Personal Affairs	111
Managing Stress	117
Health Management	123
Say Goodbye to Anger	126
Develop an Integrated Personality	130
The Goal of Human Life	134
Living with a Positive Mindset	138
Be Positive and Motivated at All Times	142

Foreword

Managing one's professional life, family life and social life without stress or tension is an art and an accomplishment. This calls for a positive outlook, a balanced mind, commitment to the profession and certain basic qualities of mind and heart. It also needs constant vigil, training and assiduous practice. The lessons for these are not imparted in our present day education system.

This book is a useful compendium of tips and guiding principles for the pursuit of excellence while managing public affairs which affect the quality of life of a large segment of people. The unique merit of this immensely readable and down-to-earth practical book is that it draws largely on self study and felt experiences of the author, as a member of the Civil Service, who had the opportunity to perform challenging administrative, judicial and developmental functions essentially linked to the well-being and happiness of the masses.

This makes the documentation of check lists practised by the author himself to near perfection. It covers a wide area of subjects like Integrity, Time Management, Assets Management, Interpersonal Relationships, Motivation, Communication and Personal Well-being. The book is distinctly different from other similar books which have a large body of theoretical content based on behavioural sciences and academic research. The personal touch greatly enhances the appeal of the book and its contents to all enlightened readers, encouraging them to put some of these ideas into practice.

Shri Rakesh K. Mittal has drawn examples and experiences largely from his days in the Government but the principles enunciated in the book have immediate relevance in diverse management environments. He has summed up the essential virtues needed by managers and householders to develop a positive attitude to deal with day-to-day vexing problems generally met with. A streak of spiritual message having universal appeal is easily discernible in the way he has concluded each chapter.

The book is of special value and relevance to young officers who have joined the administrative and other All India Services, but it is equally valuable to anyone else in their day-to-day interactions. The tips and guidelines will certainly make young managers 'sure-footed in a complex society'. The dominant message is how to serve the society better amidst conflicting environments and tempting circumstances. The author has ably brought out how health management is equally important for stress management and how a positive attitude enables one to sail through life smoothly.

The book is written in simple language and delivers his message effectively and forcefully.

My hearty congratulations to Shri Rakesh K. Mittal for distilling a large body of principles on stress-free management in such a handy and readable volume.

16 February 2006

E. Sreedharan
Managing Director
Delhi Metro Rail Corporation Ltd.

Preface

Being an officer of the Indian Administrative Service, I have been penning down my thoughts on various management issues. This was also due to the fact that I had the opportunity to serve several state PSUs (Public Sector Undertakings) as their Managing Director. Though in due course these PSUs have gone into the red, I found that if one works with some foresight and transparent sincerity they perform well and serve the intended purpose behind their creation. While there are several reasons behind their failure, one important reason is that often such opportunities are seen more for enjoying perks than for serving. In fact, this attitude is on the increase and the result is obvious. What is more unfortunate is with such an attitude not only the system suffers but the individuals too suffer equally. It results in a stressful life for most managers, thus rendering the so-called perks meaningless.

I have always considered my service and for that matter any job which provides an opportunity to serve the people or nation as a great privilege. Unfortunately, not all think on these lines. Most of us, though join our job with great enthusiasm, soon fall victim to negative thinking and stop contributing with our full potential. In the process, we not only cease to develop personally, the system also starts decaying. This is what seems to have happened today. Despite brilliant persons managing the system, there is a sense of all-round despondency. As a result, we are able to make only partial use of our potential at the individual as well as collective level.

What has really gone wrong, is a matter of detailed examination. The reasons go beyond individuals and the whole society needs to contemplate. Yet, individuals still make the difference and change things around them. The purpose of writing this book is to make these individuals realise their potential as well as their responsibilities towards the society. It is only a matter of changing our attitude. Managers, in whatsoever field they may be, set examples for others and if they display positive attitude, the process is perpetuated fast. The same is true of negative attitude too.

Having written a few books on positive approach to life, I am now humbly attempting to share my views on management in the form of this book. I have been encouraged to do so by the response given to my various write-ups in this field. Fortunately, these views are supported by real life experiences which are plenty in number. I am aware of the fact that wisdom is nobody's monopoly and more so in the field of management. The perception varies with the persons, the situation and the time. However, one thing can always be common and that is to have a positive attitude or, in other words, a problem-solving attitude. A manager who comes out with a solution to every problem is always liked over a person who comes out with a problem to every solution. It is in this background that this book may be of help.

We are well into the twenty-first century. The society, today, has become very complex and so is its expectation from managers in different fields. Therefore, today's managers need more foresight, dynamism, flexibility and transparency. Today, our positions are no more our protections; on the other hand, we need to protect our positions by our acts. The customer, today, is much more alert and demanding. In such a situation, I feel our approach to management has to change greatly. Our vision too requires more expansion and the fact is to be realised that in an interconnected society, individual's welfare also lies in the overall welfare. This calls for integrity, compassion, accessibility, knowledge, fearlessness and many other human qualities in us. These are divine qualities, which not only help in our professional excellence but also make us a better person. Thus the larger aim of life can also be achieved through better service to the people.

This reminds me of my first interaction with Mr E. Sreedharan, Managing Director of Delhi Metro Rail Corporation, when I met him in a very sublime environment of an ashram. Seeing him so relaxed I asked him about the secret of his success and that too in one line. I had put this question with great reverence and he too replied it with great affection. He said that the secret can be expressed only in one word and that word is 'INTEGRITY'. I was pleasantly amused to listen to his answer and contemplated over it for a long time. I concluded, the word 'integrity' is not a word but a textbook. Since then we have met several times and I always drew great inspiration from him. He has been very kind to write the 'foreword' of this book.

If Mr E. Sreedharan can successfully manage complicated projects like 'Konkan Railway' and 'Delhi Metro' with success and mind-boggling ease, why can't others? I feel, all of us have this capacity may be in varying degrees provided we understand and follow certain core principles of life and plan our actions accordingly. It is mainly a question of planning our resources well whether it is knowledge, intellect, talent, men, money, machinery or moments. Those who understand the power of planning do well everywhere and that too without any stress. Thus stress-free management is essentially a matter of correct understanding of core values of life and their correct application in our working.

In this small book an effort has been made to touch these aspects in a simple manner. This book has no management jargons and the expression is as much from the heart as from the head. Perhaps, right combination of them is the secret of stress-free management. Several persons, as well as institutions, have encouraged me to write this book. Many of them have been a source of my learning too. I express my deep gratitude towards all of them without mentioning their names and present this book in all humility. If it can help to bring any positive change in the system or any individual, that would be my real reward.

Last but not the least, I express my deep gratitude towards my spiritual master Swami Bhoomanand Tirtha, without whose grace this work would not have been possible.

February 2006   Rakesh K. Mittal

Our Dilemma

A big dilemma faced by a manager today is about the path to be followed by him or her. Perhaps it has always been so but now it has become a matter of serious concern. I remember to have faced this question many years back from a close friend. He raised a doubt in my mind about the use of being honest and hardworking. I had no clear answer for him. At that time I only thought that it was better to be dishonest than to regret honesty later. However, that was not out of deep conviction, and I wanted an answer which really satisfied me. That was the beginning of my search and the search was deep. I studied, discussed, contemplated and practised. Doubts came in my mind, but I continued with the process. It took me almost ten years to arrive at the conclusion that only honesty is the best path not only for society, but also for oneself. Those who are on this path are really fortunate and should have no reason to be in a dilemma.

It is easier said than done. Today's environment has become so vicious that most of us are carried away in its current. All around us is the scene of ever-growing greed for money, power and fame. Not only that, we also see gross misuse of these acquisitions. On the other hand, we see many upright and honest persons suffering for no apparent fault of theirs. We find that negative elements collude with each other easily for nefarious gains and generally succeed, while the positive elements are not able to act together. No wonder, most of us are easily tempted to believe that the path of goodness is no more in our interest.

I feel that this thinking is myopic and needs correction. It is a reality that those who shun the path of goodness are no better in terms of happiness. In fact, they are worse. The only difference is that their suffering is generally not noticed because it gets camouflaged by their outer glitter. Similarly, many subtle pleasures of good people are not visible to others. As a result wrong message emanates. After all even those who make all sorts of compromises do so only with the intention of getting more happiness. It is a different matter that they may not get it. And if happiness is the final target, then whatever route ensures this should be followed. When we take a myopic view of the situation, perhaps the path of evil may appear to be a better choice. This is what seems to be happening today. Deluded by the glamour of the outside world, we fall victim and follow a path which ultimately leads us to misery. This is happening in all walks of life, and there is hardly any exception.

When this situation comes in administration or management, it becomes a matter of even greater concern. Today's society depends on them to such an extent that its quality has a direct bearing on the people at large. Therefore, it is essential that this dilemma of ours should be removed as early as possible. Those who are wise and are able to think clearly make their mark in the long run, notwithstanding the fact that there may be temporary setbacks. It is just like losing a game but winning the match or losing a battle but winning the war. In order to come out triumphant in the war of life, there is no option but to follow the path of goodness with conviction.

The problem also arises because of the narrow definition of goodness. It is generally restricted to certain do's and don'ts. It is not so. Goodness has a much wider dimension and covers all aspects of our personality. The Bhagvad Gita mentions twenty-six qualities of a perfect man in the beginning of the sixteenth chapter. Similarly, honesty also is interpreted in a very constrictive way. This is also responsible for our dilemma. Unless we take care of all aspects of our personality, chances of suffering will always be there. In that case, it is not fair to blame our good qualities for our suffering. The fact is that we suffer because of those good qualities which we lack. Similarly, when we feel that not so good people are gainers, it may be due to some of the qualities in them which we may be lacking. Also, there is something called luck or destiny on which we have no control except doing our best in the present so as to create a better destiny for the future.

Having realised this fact, our effort should be to cultivate missing qualities rather than to give up the existing qualities. Once our personality becomes integrated in a true sense, no amount of temptation can deviate us from the path of virtue and our dilemma disappears completely. We then gladly accept all situations of life and enjoy them fully. Administration or management too then becomes a very natural and stress-free process.

Let us, therefore, make an effort in this direction. It is worth the effort and sacrifice, if at all, it is so. I can assure that if we do so, the gain will certainly be more than the pain.

The Missing Dimension

After more than fifty years of Independence, the Indian bureaucracy is now standing at crossroads facing an uncertain future because of sweeping national and international changes. Particularly in the past few years, the whole approach and direction of the Government and the political and economic thinking in India has undergone a vast change which had not been imagined. It now depends on us whether to give up or mould ourselves according to the needs of the time. The British left us with a well-established bureaucracy which was efficient, professional and, to a great extent, incorruptible. Fortunately, this legacy continues largely even today, but the decay is fast. Despite this, the need of this steel frame is still there but with certain corrections. If we don't awaken to this reality soon, the day may not be far when we become redundant.

This should make us think about the missing dimension in general, and as administrators in particular. Today, the field of administration has grown so vast that hardly any aspect of human life remains untouched. The fulfilment of our most basic needs of food, clothing and shelter greatly depends on the effectiveness of administration. Even our personal life is influenced by Government policies in many ways. For example, the size of our family is guided by the Government policy in this regard and a divorce is decided by judicial administration. What is meant is that today we come in contact with the administration in almost all aspects of life. Whether it is education, travel, power supply, water supply, entertainment, communication, agriculture, industrial and business activity, investment of our savings or any other activity of life, the quality of administrative machinery has a direct bearing on the quality of our lives. The purpose of administration is to make life better and equitable to the extent possible. It was expected that the Government system, being neutral and welfare-oriented, would work in the true spirit of trusteeship and the benefits of economic development would be shared by all. However, what seems to have happened is just the opposite. Neither have we developed to the extent that the benefits would reach all in a natural manner, nor have we been able to develop efficient and effective regulatory mechanism. No wonder, the result is what we see today. What is worse is the fact that this failure on the part of administration is making our nation pessimistic with hardly any zeal for future. In view of this the subject requires serious contemplation.

It is a matter of satisfaction that concern for this failure is being felt and shown by many of those who are supposed to be responsible for it. Several steps have been and are being taken also. Some of them have yielded good results but overall the impact has not been significant. For example, having seen the failure of public sector in general, a policy of liberalisation was adopted with great hopes. The same has hardly helped the economy as the areas vital to growth remained mostly in the public sector. The necessary private investment did not come mainly because we failed to provide an administrative machinery which could implement such policy changes in an effective manner. We are still bogged down in rules and regulations and fail to see our role in totality. Above this, the sharp fall in human values has made the system even more unfit to deliver the goods. Therefore, any effort to change the situation should take care of both the aspects, i.e., the correct policies and their honest implementation.

Where have we failed despite our realisation of the problem and wish to overcome it ? This is a question which haunts or should haunt all those who are seriously concerned with the future of our nation. Mere talks or cosmetic changes are not going to help much. This we have tried enough and need not emphasise any more. Unless we have a keen desire and strong will to change things for the better, not much purpose is served by any discussion on the subject. Most of us raise this issue almost every day in our drawing-rooms, coffee-rooms and even in the offices. But that is mainly to justify our inefficiency and deviation rather than due to any serious concern. This makes things even worse and we end up as a more pessimistic lot. First of all this should stop. All negative thoughts should be eschewed. Fifty years is not a very long period in the life of a nation, though it may be so for an individual. The last fifty years have particularly appeared long because of rapid advance in science and technology. It is said that the scientific progress in these fifty years has been more than the progress achieved in the last 2,000 years. As a result, the internal development of man has not been able to keep pace with external development. Most of us have got so much involved in this progress that the finer aspects of life have been missed. We thought that the material progress would provide answer to all our problems. The present dilemma is due to the falsification of this expectation.

We now come to the basic definition of the word 'progress' particularly in reference to mankind. For most of us, material progress has become the sole criterion of 'progress'. All our policies are also directed towards meeting this criterion. In the process, the administrative system or the management which is supposed to implement the policies, has also come to believe in the same definition of progress and has developed its culture accordingly. This is, however, a very incomplete view of progress. Material progress, no doubt, is important in the welfare of mankind but the same is only a means and not an end in itself. The end is universal happiness, love, peace and sense of fulfilment. This end cannot be achieved merely by material progress but requires mutual understanding and concern also. Without them material progress is incomplete and fails to provide true happiness which we all are trying to seek.

This is where we have gone wrong. Those who believe that mere material achievement will provide them happiness, make all sorts of compromises but eventually fail to achieve the objective. By the time they realise their mistake, generally it is too late and their frustration is passed on to society. We seem to be passing through this phase but unfortunately are yet to seek the right solution. The mistake being committed is that we expect others to change first, and since everyone is expecting the same way, any solution eludes us. In the process, we start believing that values don't work while also admitting in the same breath that absence of values is playing havoc with the society. Those few who are able to see the situation in the right perspective, though make a difference around them, have become a miserable minority in the overall system. No wonder, in due course, many of them also get frustrated. The situation has, therefore, reached such a critical state that we all are confused and also desperate to change. I consider it as a sign of hope.

With this background, we come to the missing dimension in administration or management and I consider policy-makers also as a part of them. Policy and its implementation are complementary to each other and they cannot be seen in isolation. Our policies need to be directed towards the goal of integrated progress and should take care of external as well as internal needs of mankind. Similarly, in the implementation of policies, human beings should not be considered as merely numbers or objects. It should be remembered that rules and regulations are made for human beings and not vice versa. Therefore, they should be interpreted with a human touch. When we do so in good faith and with honesty, chances of disharmony are reduced greatly and the whole environment becomes conducive to growth as well as peace, happiness and love. Such a process has a multiplying effect, turning frustration into inspiration and enthusiasm. What we seek to achieve through wrong means and fail is then achieved effortlessly. Living thus becomes a pleasure and eventually everyone feels happy. Actually heaven and hell are nothing but synonyms of cooperation and the lack of it.

What do we call this missing dimension? I would like to call it the 'Human Dimension' or the 'Spiritual Dimension'. Only when we see each other as human beings or part of the same spirit, we develop mutual love and compassion. The cooperation then comes naturally and selfishness goes away. Once we are selfless, the need of deviating from values does not arise and we see our welfare in the welfare of all. After all, nothing belongs to us. All material possessions, in ultimate analysis, belong to Nature and are meant for sharing as per our need. Nature has enough provision for our needs. When sharing is equitable, ill-will towards each other does not arise, and we all get our share without any need of pouncing on it. In that situation, the gains of science and technology can also be used to enhance happiness through comfortable living.

Those who, by destiny, have been entrusted to manage the resources of Nature should consider themselves fortunate and take it as a rare opportunity. If managers look at their jobs with this attitude, the missing dimension will reveal itself effortlessly. The fact is that our basic nature is of truth, love and cooperation. These virtues come to us naturally while deviation from them needs effort. For too long, we have lived as slaves and this has made us forget our basic nature. The British administrative system had different objectives and these are not applicable to a free developing nation in toto. While a good deal has to be learnt from them, what is to be remembered is that we are serving our own people and nation. This is what we have been forgetting hitherto.

Let us not forget human sciences in the glamour of material sciences. They are complementary to each other and neglect of any will be at the cost of human progress and happiness. While the call of Swami Vivekanand at the turn of the nineteenth century was to use material sciences to support spiritual sciences in order to eradicate physical poverty, the need at the turn of the twentieth century is that spiritual sciences should come in support of material sciences in order to eradicate mental poverty. That only will ensure integrated development of the society as well as the individual. In this agenda, managers in fields have a key role to play provided they realise this missing dimension.

The Human Element in Management

It is true that most of those who join administrative or management services are intelligent and brilliant in their academic careers. Very soon they acquire necessary knowledge of the rules, procedures and technical skills essential for their job. However, not all are equally successful in their careers. While many factors are responsible for this difference, one major factor is the human element, which counts more than anything else. No matter how institutionalised the system may become, the individual who occupies the chair makes all the difference. The fact is that our human qualities are the most precious possessions which we must never lose. In this chapter certain tips are being given which may help in maintaining our human qualities in all possible situations. These are as follows:

- It should be realised and accepted with conviction that any administrative system is for the people and not the other way round. If we believe in this, many misgivings will go on their own and our basic human qualities will start growing in an effortless manner. If we visualise the affected person behind every action of ours, our objectivity and interpretation of the situation will improve automatically.
- While it is essential to acquire technical and managerial skill, it should be remembered that for an administrator, the conceptual skill is most important. And for the development of the same, human factor is very important. Unless he is a good human being, it is not possible for him to become a good manager or a good leader.

- Whether superiors, subordinates, colleagues, officers of other departments or members of the public—all are human beings full of likes and dislikes, secret resentments and cherished ambitions. Success depends on how you conduct yourself and get along with them. You have to deal with men and matters, not just papers.
- Even the ablest of persons cannot do everything alone. Team effort and team spirit is always required. Your own hard work is of course important, but organisational and institutional base is essential. The most successful men are not those who burn the midnight oil themselves, but are able to lead, guide and inspire others to work for them. The one who is able to arouse enthusiasm is the one headed for leadership.
- Sincerity and integrity are two qualities which count most in inspiring persons around you. Sincerity is the most important quality and is infectious too. It is even most important from the point of view of personal happiness in life. Similarly, if integrity is not there, you can never guide or inspire others. Without integrity you will attract not respect but contempt.
- Avoid cynical and critical approach in your working. In every person, situation or decision, it is possible to find the positive as well as the negative. It depends upon your attitude to dwell on any of the two. When you dwell on the positive, results are amazing and the negative starts disappearing. Same is the case when you dwell on the negative. While corrective actions are required to take care of the negative, the gain of the positive should not be lost in the process.
- While dealing with the officials and members of the public, even little courtesies go a long way. In offering chairs, returning greetings, phrasing instructions in a polite and courteous manner, using 'Please' and 'Thank You', etc., you hardly spend anything but gain a lot. At times, at the call of duty you may have to sacrifice a person for a purpose, but it should never be for a petty or ordinary purpose.

The Human Element in Management

- The personal problems of your staff must command your first sympathy. Lack of accommodation in small matters like joining time, TA bills, casual leave, withdrawals from the GPF, etc., can have far-reaching consequences and adversely affect the morale. Therefore, pettiness should be avoided and fullest accommodation and understanding should be shown.
- Give full credit for work well done. One of the deepest urges in human nature is the craving to be appreciated. Give plentiful of it. Nothing builds up a person so much as approbation and appreciation.
- All of us realise the difference when we have to deal with the man behind the counter. Keep this in mind when you are the man behind the table.
- A smiling face does wonders. It has been rightly said that a man without a smiling face should not open a shop. When we meet a person with a smile on our face, half of his trouble goes away without expressing it. The chances are that he will go back satisfied even if we are not able to help him as per his expectations.
- A character role is as much a picture of the person writing it as the person written upon. It should be written after full consideration and reflection. Avoid little shortcomings. Pull up then and there, sharply if necessary, but do not blot the permanent record. Give as much credit as possible and stress all good points. Defects and shortcomings should be mentioned only after due warning, if the person proves incorrigible and intractable.
- It should also be remembered that goodness alone is not sufficient. By being merely good, you may be loved but may not be obeyed. A manager can hardly afford such a situation. Therefore, when insincerity of a person is clear, you must be severe. Even when excusing, put things down in writing. Let it hang like a sword of Damocles over his head. Writing will also come in useful in self-defence if counter accusations are made against you.

- Sometimes when nothing else works, it might be a good strategy that when a person is repeatedly at fault, to blow up his immediate superior. Thereafter, that superior will be very sure to look after his erring subordinates.
- There is nothing more important for an administrator than to have the capacity for decision-making. Readiness to take decisions is something you must never loose. Also, the decisions taken should be clear and firm. There should be no scope of double interpretation. The tendency of writing 'Please Speak' should be minimal and only when a genuine discussion is called for. It should never be for the sake of avoiding decisions or for passing on the responsibility.
- At times it is good to form committees to take decisions in certain matters. It helps in getting wiser counsel and also the consensus. However, it should not be used as a tool for avoiding responsibility. Quite often the decision taken through committees gets delayed and the purpose is defeated. It has been rightly said that a committee is a gathering of gentlemen who singly can do nothing, but collectively decide that nothing can be done.
- To be really successful to build up the team, you must delegate powers. But while delegation of powers should be the maximum, always keep your eyes open and hands on the controls. For this, hard work in the early stages of your career is the key to success. It will give you the mastery which will enable you later to assess what is happening instead of having to go through the details yourself. But occasionally, you must be prepared to go into great details. The staff members will then be on the alert.
- Coordination should be done with the least show of authority. The steel should always be beneath the velvet. Only that coordination is worth having, which is based on willing cooperation. Give everyone the due sense of importance. This is also one of the deepest urges in human nature. Do not be ruffled by opposition and obstruction. A successful

man is the one who can lay a firm foundation with the bricks that others throw at him.

- Relations with your colleagues are very important and may be difficult at times. Everyone should be respected and given due recognition. Departmental sensitivities and jealousies have to be handled with diplomatic skill. Family and spouse also play an important role in one's relation with one's colleagues.

- Perhaps the most difficult relationship of all is the relationship with superiors. Here you are at a disadvantage. Qualities that a superior is entitled to expect are sincerity to work and loyalty to him. Loyalty is even more important. If this relationship cannot be established, better be frank about it and try to get yourself transferred away (not him). If you try to get him transferred and fail, then all hell will break loose. Also remember that a bad superior can be a blessing in disguise and may teach you to be alert and wary. So if you cannot move out, then face the situation with this in mind.

- Insofar as personal and social relationship with superiors is concerned, a respectful distance should always be maintained. By doing so, you will not arouse envy or resentment of colleagues, will not embarrass the superior if he is keen to help you, will not be loaded with extra work and will not run the risk of incurring his displeasure. Also never resort to flattery. Listen attentively and respectfully to what a superior says, and this in itself will please him.

- Be accessible to the members of public. Give an opportunity for people blowing off steam at your level rather than higher up. In the process of meeting people, you derive valuable information. Fix some time in office when anyone can come to you. While meeting people, be always firm and fair but also tactful and polite. There is a way of saying 'No' that does not give offence. You must be able to give a sense of satisfaction to people, even if you do not do all that they want.

- Do not seclude yourself in an ivory tower. Go out and meet the people. The more you mix with them, the more you will be enthused and strengthened. Likewise, participation in the religious, social or family functions is of great help in building good and meaningful relationships. Of course, it is essential to discriminate between right and wrong people.
- Relations with politicians are very important. As the people's representatives they are entitled to be treated with courtesy and respect. Their suggestions can be quite useful at times. Tendency to rule them out or view them with suspicion just because they come from politicians must be overcome. They are aware of the double standards we apply and resent them. Above all, we should be absolutely impartial while dealing with politicians. Departure from this is the one thing they will not forgive. We must never allow ourselves to be manoeuvred into a position where we have to rely on one party or group. At the same time do not become their tool which may eventually be used against you.
- Almost the same is true with the minister. Your minister is entitled to expect absolute loyalty and sincerity. You may or may not agree with his views but there should never be double standards. What you feel to be correct should be expressed honestly but once a decision has been taken by him it must be complied with sincerely. If he is not correct, in all probability, the finance, the law or the personnel department will take care of it. Nowadays, even courts come in the way. As a mature administrator, the compulsions of a minister should also be given due allowance.
- The golden rule in dealing with the press is to let your achievements be such that they come to you, rather than you go to them. The relationship has to be very balanced, neither too close nor too distant. The press has a very important role to play and this should be duly respected. Whatever be the aberration, it still holds true that if you are right, the press cannot fiddle with you beyond a point and will soon become objective in its reporting. If there is any exception, it should be ignored too.

- A manager has to be adaptable. You may not be able to do all that you consider good, but as long as you do not do anything you know to be bad, you should be reasonably satisfied. Rigidity will hurt you, even if you are in the right. Learn flexibility from the tree that bows before every blast and comes upright again.
- As far as possible avoid display of temper. Remember 'ANGER' is just one letter short of 'DANGER'. It may put you hopelessly in the wrong where you may be absolutely in the right. Words once spoken can never be erased. Therefore, you have to be very watchful against losing temper. It is a different matter that at times a show of temper is necessary for strategic reasons.
- One important human element is the willingness to depart from the beaten track and set procedures, when the situation demands it. It is the greatest of all mistakes to do nothing because you can only do a little. While departing, even if you make a mistake, there is always a chance for you. What we call failure is not the falling down, but the staying down.
- Last but not the least, your own effort is all important. Genius is said to be one part inspiration and nine parts perspiration. In our own humble manner, let our actions speak louder than words and our own conduct be an example and inspiration for others to follow. Again and again, you will come across situations of great disappointment, depression, despair and desolation. But never lose heart and remember that winners are those who persevere when all the rest give up.

Positive Thinking for Excellence

We are passing through a period when the course of nature is exposing the misdeeds of many of us who are or have been at the helm of affairs of public administration or management. To some, this situation may appear to be gloomy, but I see it totally from a positive point of view. To me, it is an indication of the fact that if we fail to look at ourselves, Nature will create conditions to compel us to do so and it may be doing so through some of us only; may be holding different positions in the society. This is exactly what is happening now. One should not, therefore, feel dejected in such a situation. This is more true in the field of administration upon which depends the larger welfare of the society. I am of the view that today, administrative excellence can be achieved by adopting a positive approach in our working.

Before I go deeper into the subject, I would like to explain the first two words of the topic. The first word is 'Positive'. I consider this word to be a symbol of growth in a larger sense. It is not different from the word 'Yoga' which means addition and communion. It is something which elevates, enriches, enlarges, expands and contributes to our growth. It has no place for selfishness, narrowness, mental poverty, parochialism, etc. A person with a positive approach thinks in a larger perspective and for greater prosperity. He does not do so as a matter of charity and believes it to be in his interest too. After all, one is a part of the whole and can survive only as long as the whole survives. He gives only to receive, may be in a different form, because he understands that when looked in totality, there is no difference between giving and receiving, and it is only a matter of exchange. Thus his approach is always growth-oriented and this is what I consider to be positive.

The second word 'Thinking' is also equally important. After all, the process of thinking is what differentiates man from animals. It is a wonderful faculty provided by God to human beings. And it is the quality of thinking which distinguishes one person from another. Our best friends and our worst enemies are our thoughts and they make or mar the whole dignity of a person. Every action begins with a thought. As are the thoughts, so are the actions.

With this background, it becomes easier to understand the phrase 'Positive Thinking' as something growth-oriented, taking a larger perspective and greater happiness as the goals. Here an individual is a part of the whole and the gain of the whole automatically becomes the gain of the individual. When a larger number of people adopt this approach, there is greater prosperity and happiness in the society. In the process, it elevates an individual also and brings him closer to the true goal of life. I see no difference between positive thinking and value-based thinking. It may also be called spiritual thinking because it is the soul that thinks, in accordance with its 'Sanskars' through its faculty of intellect. When one thinks of spiritual growth, larger growth is automatically implied.

The concept of positive thinking is important in all aspects of life and for all people. It brings about both external as well as internal growth. A person may be rich or poor but positive thinking makes his life better irrespective of his material possessions. I shall now try to relate the concept of positive thinking with managerial excellence.

We are living in a period which can easily be called one of the most challenging humanity has seen thus far. The scientific growth has taken place at a mind-boggling pace which has created a gulf between the inner growth and the outer growth of an individual, as well as the society. The expectations of a civilised democratic society have grown so much that they pose a great challenge before its managers, be they in the field of politics, administration or business. It, therefore, becomes very essential that they are able to meet such a challenge and I feel that positive thinking endows them with the capability to do so. It is my experience that a clear concept of life and its values are of great help in the field of management leading to excellence, contentment, satisfaction and fulfilment in life. These concepts are, in other words, nothing but 'Positive Thoughts'. I shall now cover some of them to prove their relevance in the field of management.

Integrity

The foremost requirement for effective management is the integrity of the manager. It is also necessary to understand the full dimension of the quality called 'integrity'. The dictionary meaning of this word is entireness, wholeness, the unimpaired state, uprightness, honesty, purity, etc. In a way it covers almost all qualities of a good human being and is much more than the normally understood meaning of the word. A manager, while discharging his duty, is supposed to have a complete view of the situation without being influenced by external factors and take upright decision with a pure and honest mind. This is what encompasses the quality called integrity. Therefore, any deviation from this would mean loss of integrity. It is, therefore, necessary to understand all possible factors which help us in maintaining our integrity and assimilate them in us to avoid loss of integrity. In my view, these factors are nothing but positive thoughts, which help us to take a positive view of every situation and this gives us more satisfaction than what would apparently come from the loss of integrity. My personal experience is that fifty per cent of our problems as administrators or managers are taken care of, if we maintain our integrity in a true sense. This is possible only by developing a positive approach towards life and by looking at it in totality rather than taking a lop-sided view. One should also work with full integrity not by compulsion but by choice. That only will lead to management excellence.

Knowledge

Knowledge is the second most important requirement of a successful manager. Knowledge is power and without it, it is difficult to command true respect from others; it is, therefore, absolutely essential that we know our job well and master it as early as possible. It does not mean that there is need for knowing each and everything, but definitely, the essentials should be known. It is also important that we keep a learning attitude and do not hesitate to learn from others irrespective of their status. This willingness to learn itself earns respect for us. At the same time, we must respect the knowledge of others and our position should not come in the way of appreciating others. The attitude of mutual respect is very essential in management and if we do so, we shall not only be obeyed but will be respected too.

Trust

Trust is another important factor necessary for excellence. This is possible when we accept the fact that each person is potentially divine, and if the right environment is provided to him, he will show his excellence. Trusting is one of the important components of this environment. Only a person who is confident of himself can trust others. Thus trusting by itself is a divine quality. We must accept the fact that there is an inner urge in each of us to perform our best and we can do so only when we are trusted, and we, in turn, trust all those who work with us or are under us. It may be clarified here that trusting does not at all mean 'not being careful'. That one has always to be. Even while one walks on the road, one has to be careful. This does not mean that one should not walk on the road. My personal experience is that trusting is very rarely harmful while non-trusting is always so. A manager, at times, has to deal with negative and wicked elements. My feeling is that an environment of trusting brings a positive change in them also, and if there are some exceptions, they can always be dealt with strongly. The only care to be taken is that strong action should be taken as a call of duty and not as vendetta.

Accessibility

A manager or administrator has to deal with a large number of people both inside and outside the organisation. They come to him for various official as well as personal matters. An effective administrator has to be accessible within reasonable parameters. I am of the view that this accessibility itself is able to take care of a good number of his problems and gives much fewer occasions to negative elements to play mischief. Unfortunately, many of us get trapped by vested interests in such a manner that we are distanced from reality and get a version of things which is far away from truth. Such a caucus should be broken with wisdom and courage. Many happenings, which we see around today, are the result of lack of accessibility. Even a person with genuine intentions may fall victim to the designs of vested interests, if he is not wise enough. Again, it is a result of positive thinking which helps us in remaining accessible to those who need us. As a manager or administrator, if we consider it a privilege to be of service to others, we can always find time and occasion to meet those who come to us. My experience is that a common man or employee gives the best feedback which an effective administrator can use for larger interest. The mere fact that you love meeting others instils confidence among the people and leads to administrative excellence.

Compassion

Compassion is more than mercy. It is putting oneself in the position of the person in trouble. When one does so, he becomes more considerate and helpful. Definitely, it does not mean being sentimental which may take away the objectivity. For an effective manager or administrator, compassion is a great quality. With compassion, one is able to help others without necessarily helping. Compassion imparts dignity to a person in trouble. Quite often, we are not able to help others, but by compassion, we show our willingness to help. This does wonders in administration. My experience is that with compassion, even severe punishment is accepted gracefully and it does good to the person on whom the punishment is inflicted. On the other hand, even rewards may have no meaning if given with indifference. Again, compassion is a quality which comes as a result of positive thinking or spiritual development and helps greatly in achieving excellence.

Fearlessness

Fear is a big hurdle in the effectiveness of a manager, be it for any reason. Positive thinking helps in winning over this fear. Be it the fear of survival or anything else, it takes away the objectivity of a person and in all probability leads to loss of integrity. A positive thinker always takes things in their stride and sees an opportunity for development in every situation. Once we accept things as they come, the cause of fear itself disappears. Not only this, a fearless administrator is able to instil fear among the wicked which either makes them behave properly or keeps them away from the scene. This imparts more confidence among the good people and the process perpetuates itself. There are ample examples which show that it is possible to show courage even when most of the system is against you. Once courage is shown, things change fast in your favour. However, in the process, humility should not be lost. In fact, humility is an ornament of the courageous person and it should never be confused with weakness. On the other hand, it adds to the strength of the bold. Qualities like courage and humility are also the result of positive thinking.

Patience

Patience is another important quality of an effective administrator. After all, he works in an environment which is not always favourable. One comes across many unreasonable persons, situations and events. He has to deal with them with patience. Loss of temper is highly detrimental in such situations. At times, it may be necessary to convey displeasure with firmness. But quite often, it is patience which pays rich dividends. Not all administrative problems have an immediate answer and take time for solution. A good manager does not spend undue time and energy on such problems. He also has the necessary wisdom to identify such problems. This approach is again positive thinking and greatly helps in achieving excellence. However, one thing is certain—good intention and efforts definitely lead to good results, though it may take a little longer at times. One should also remember that the path to success is through the staircase and not through the elevator. Success achieved this way is long-lasting too.

Acceptance

There is a well-known saying 'Accept what you cannot change'. There is lot of wisdom in it. I am of the view that, if understood correctly, this approach leads to excellence in all spheres of life, and administration is no exception. We live in an environment which has a great variety. It is not necessary to reach a consensus or to give one answer to all the problems. Perceptions change with persons, situation and time. Our perception may be different from others and we may not be in a position to act as per our perception. In such a situation, it is wise to accept a different viewpoint if it is in the larger interest. A good administrator is supposed to have this kind of flexibility. He does not make an issue which can be avoided and there is no question of thinking in terms of self-prestige. Quite often, flexibility brings us more prestige than rigidity. For excellence in administration, flexibility is an important requirement and this is again part of positive thinking. Here, one should remember the following:

For every malady under the Sun,
There is a remedy, or there is none.
If there is one, go try and find it,
If there is none, then never mind it.

These lines sum up the whole concept of acceptance and need no further explanation.

There may be many other attributes of a positive administrator. I am not going into them. The field of administration is very wide and there is no definite answer to every problem. However, with a general positive approach, it is possible to face all situations gracefully leading to a larger welfare. This approach in itself is sufficient to achieve the true goal of life. Sometimes a question arises in our minds. Does positive thinking always work? Of course it does. Positive thinking will work if we are willing to work at it. It is not an easy discipline. It takes hard work and a strong belief. It also requires honest living and a keen desire to succeed. We need to keep working at it constantly to achieve success. Just when we believe, we have mastered it, we will have to develop it, again. However, success could be available to all of us if we follow these basic principles of positive thinking.

Integrity

Today, integrity is a much talked about word, particularly in public life. All public servants are supposed to have integrity beyond doubt. A certificate is also supposed to be given to every civil servant about his integrity. And most of them get the certificates. But can we say that the integrity of civil servants, in general, is beyond doubt or even satisfactory for that matter? If not, it has to be deeply analysed.

Before we do so, the word 'integrity' should itself be properly understood. The normal meaning given to this word is 'Not Taking Bribes'. The Chambers Dictionary meaning of this word is— entireness; wholeness; the unimpaired state of anything; uprightness; honesty; purity. Obviously, 'Integrity' is a much wider term than what is normally understood.

A manager, while discharging his duties, is supposed to have a complete view of the situation without being influenced by external factors and taking an upright decision with pure and honest mind. This is what can be an ideal definition of the quality called 'integrity'. Therefore, any deviation from this would mean loss of integrity. 'Bribe' is one factor, though a prominent one, which is likely to cause deviation. But other factors also cause deviation. These may be fear of survival, caste consideration, prejudice, vendetta, suspicion, over-ambition, etc. Deviation from correct decision due to any of these factors also means loss of integrity. Then there are factors like misuse of power, wastage of resources, etc., which are generally overlooked. There is need for suitable checks in these areas also.

Unfortunately, our system has miserably failed to check this evil despite many administrative measures. This is mainly because 'integrity' is basically a 'state of mind' which cannot be influenced much only by administrative measures. It is a sum total of the influences of various factors and in a way reflects the state of the society. There can always be found a counter to any administrative measure. Such measures will be effective only when there is influence at the mental level also. Otherwise, those who have already deviated will keep on deviating more and more while administrative measures will remain in force for those who do not need them.

Therefore, the role of those in a superior position in all walks of life (not merely public services) becomes important. Indian people, by and large, are a satisfied lot and happily accept their condition provided the leaders of society show their integrity. Unfortunately, it has not been the case and the result is obvious. The old principle, that one should not only be clean but also appear clean, has been grossly misused. The entire emphasis has shifted to appearing clean rather than being clean. Many do not care even to appear clean. Obvious corruption charges are refuted by responsible persons on the ground that the charges are not proved. Many times they don't even care to say that charges are wrong. And all of us know how difficult it is to prove such charges. In such a state of affairs, it is no use blaming lesser mortals and applying administrative measures to them. In fact, those who are supposed to apply these measures are themselves not above board. Thus, the exercise becomes all the more futile.

There is need for establishing that corruption ultimately leads to unhappiness in the society at large. To begin with, some people may feel happy at the cost of others, but a stage comes when everyone becomes a victim of the system. In the present age of science and technology, this will have to be established in a logical manner. All people may not understand the science of our scriptures which plead for right conduct. There have to be economic and social explanations of the havoc that corruption plays with the society. It should be established that, if we do not mend our ways, the whole society will have to pay the price.

Fortunately, the roots of our society are deep and strong. So far the damage refers to our values, it can be said to be only surface damage. The people of India, by and large, are a God-fearing satisfied lot. At the same time, they are aware of their strength. Those in high places should not take them for granted. If they do not mend their ways gracefully, people will force them to do so. This is where the hope lies. Let us hope that all those in responsible positions will work with full 'integrity' not by compulsion but by choice. The rest of the society will automatically follow them. In that event, administrative measures can also be taken effectively against the defaulters. In this agenda, the role of administrators and managers is very important.

Plan Your Money

These days rarely do we find a person who is happy within his income. It is true that prices have been going up at a fast rate but so have incomes. I don't mean to say that prices have not adversely affected the common man. But I definitely do not consider this the only reason for being unhappy with what most of us get. I believe that in most of the cases, there is enough money and it depends on us how wisely we use it without sacrificing the essential needs of life.

The late Swami Chinmayanandji, used to describe the 'Happiness Index' as the ratio of 'number of desires fulfilled' and 'number of desires entertained'. That is:

$$\text{Happiness Index} = \frac{\text{Number of desires fulfilled}}{\text{Number of desires entertained}}$$

There can be two ways of raising this index, i.e., by increasing the numerator or decreasing the denominator. The trouble with most of us is that as the number of desires fulfilled increases, the number of desires entertained also increases at a much faster rate. This results in a fall in the value of the 'Happiness Index'. With this kind of approach, it will never be possible to raise the Happiness Index, no matter what may be the increase in our income or resources. So if the index is to be raised, at least the denominator should remain constant. The better way of raising the index would be to decrease the number of desires entertained, once our essential needs are fulfilled. The index will become infinite, if the number of desires is reduced to zero. That is to say that a person having no desire is the happiest person. I, however, have no intention of advocating such a state of mind.

This analysis brings us to the conclusion that if we want to be happy within our means, we have to reduce our needs and desires. To do so, we shall have to rationally analyse our present needs with an open mind. And if we do so, I am sure that there will be many areas in which money can be saved without discomfort. Broadly, the needs and desires can be classified into three categories—essential needs, comfort needs and luxury needs.

Fulfilment of essential needs is necessary for survival. Food, clothing, shelter, education and health care fall in this category. Among these, food is the most important. One need not give many arguments to establish that there can be a wide range of expenditure on all these essential needs. However, one should believe in the basic fact that Nature has given us enough for our needs but not for our greed. That being so, it depends upon us as to how we spend on these essential needs. For example, when we talk of food, the main criteria should be the nutrition and we all know that nutritious food is not necessarily costly. In all probability, it will be the other way round. For example, seasonal and fresh fruits/vegetables are generally the cheapest and most nutritious. All food items, if properly planned in terms of requirements and timings, can save a lot of money. The same is the case with clothing. Here the main criteria should be decency and convenience. Costly dresses are not always decent. Also maintaining more than a reasonable number of dresses is not only expensive but also inconvenient. One can easily establish norms of adding new dresses and at the same time, helping the poor people by giving them the old dresses.

As far as shelter is concerned, it is more difficult to draw a line. At the same time, it is one of the major items of expenditure. Unfortunately, in our country, the concept of constructing functional house is missing fast and in most of the cases money is spent for the sake of spending. There is vast scope for saving money in the construction of houses without sacrificing comfort, nay, with more comfort. It is, mainly because of the extravagance of those who have excessive money, that the construction of house is becoming more and more difficult for the common man. Those who construct houses with limited resources should try to be as functional as possible. The main criteria should be proper light, ventilation and safety. Those who go for rented house should also look for these features. A small, well-kept house is always better appreciated than an ill-kept big one.

Similar planning is required in the field of education and health care. These also vary widely in terms of quality and cost. Expenditure on education can be saved by proper selection of school, proper attention on children and efficient use of aids. In case of health care, the attention should be more on prevention than cure. These days there is too much emphasis on costly medicines. It may not always be possible to avoid them but most of the time one can manage with an economical treatment.

Having met the essential needs, one should properly plan the needs falling in the category of comfort. Items like television, refrigerator, means of transport, etc., may be said to fall in this category for most of the middle-class families. There is more scope for showing wisdom in this area and one should understand his limitations well. In no case should one stretch these needs beyond one's means.

The last category of needs is luxury needs. These may be called 'Desires', and the Happiness Index mainly depends upon them. One desire generally leads to another and there is no end to them. Hence, there is need to be careful right from the beginning, otherwise one ends up losing not only money but mental peace too. Therefore, luxury needs should always be given up. In all probability 'Desires' take away one's happiness in the long run, if not immediately. The interesting thing is that individually most of us feel that extravagance is bad but somehow we keep on indulging in it. Therefore, need is to get away from this cycle. But someone has to make the beginning. Why not we?

A good technique to plan expenditure is to ask two questions whenever a need is felt in mind. One, whether it is essential, and if it is not, drop it then and there. In case it turns out to be essential, the next question should be whether it can be postponed. If yes, it should be postponed. Most likely it will become non-essential during the period of postponement. If, even after that, it remains essential and immediate, it should be fulfilled. Frequent visits to market should be avoided. Many non-essential needs become essential when you go around the market. As far as possible one should go to the market with a definite list of items on a piece of paper or in mind and confine one's purchase to that.

Thus, if a man keeps control over his desires and spends his resources wisely on essential personal and social needs, there will be no occasion for complaining. And, if society at large is able to do so, even the bad shape of the economy, which we see today, will improve. And then most of us will start believing that there is enough money.

Plan Your Time

We generally talk of only three resources, namely, 'Man', 'Money' and 'Material'. I add a fourth resource to it, namely, 'Moments' or 'Time'. I consider time to be a very important resource which should be managed even more effectively. This is so because lost moments never come back.

The importance of time management is supreme for managers who remain busy in multifarious activities. If they do not manage their time well, they end up sitting very late in the office and thus disturbing their personal life also. Not only so, when they do not work as per schedule, time of so many other persons like subordinates, customers, public, etc., is wasted. My experience is that it is not correct to complain about shortage of time. It is only a matter of planning it well. If we do plan our time well, we shall have time for all necessary activities. Therefore, for effective time management, it is essential to develop this consciousness of the value of time as a resource, and consequently, the need for its proper management.

Next step is time-budgeting. More than money, time is to be budgeted properly. First, draw up an annual plan with regard to all important business and personal items. Every quarter, draw up a fairly detailed plan for the quarter. Every month-end, draw up a plan for the following month and so with the week. Every day, in the morning, plan in detail the day's activities. Time spent in all this planning will be rewarded back in the form of better efficiency. Various models can be drawn up for daily time-budget and one can choose according to his convenience.

The approach to time management should be an integrated one. It has to take into account all aspects of your daily life. However, for purpose of discussion, time can be divided into three aspects—Biological Time, Business or Office Time and Social Time. The general principles of these aspects shall be discussed here in order to make the best use of time.

Biological Time

Your body is the instrument of work and should be kept in very good order. Biological needs like sleep, food and recreation should, therefore, be well regulated. Time management with regard to these biological needs, therefore, assumes great significance. There are four general principles of Biological Time Management.

- Treat all days alike. Treating some days as holidays and some others as working days upsets the routine. If you get up at the same time and complete ablution and other daily necessities, you will get a complete grip on the entire day.
- In all repetitive activities, find out time-saving efficiency techniques. For instance, even if you save five minutes every day in bathing or shaving, you will be saving thirty hours in a year!
- Regulate your daily activities in a clock-like fashion. It means that, by and large, there should be fixed time for your biological activities like food, exercise, sleep, etc.
- It is advisable to develop the habit of getting up early in the morning. It has several advantages. The mind is fresh and powerful. There are no disturbances. The environment is quiet and you can work with tremendous concentration. However, those who cannot get up early, should develop the habit of staying awake late at night. But it is certain that two hours of early morning are much more than two hours of late night, in terms of efficiency.

Business Time

Time spent in office or at business place is known as Business Time and is obviously very important. There are some general principles governing Business Time. They are:

- Feel healthy and cheerful when you are in office or at business place. If you don't feel so, it may be advisable to stay at home and take rest. Your irritation in office could cost very dearly.
- Reach your workplace well in time and if possible, little before time. This changes the whole atmosphere of the office and in all likelihood, you will be able to leave office in time in the evening also. The day's output of the whole office will also increase tremendously.
- Structure your office time suitably depending upon your needs. However, the structure should be able to take care of unforeseen situations. This is necessary to avoid irritation when such situation appears.
- Make best use of your support services like telephone, computer, intercom, fax machine, personal staff, etc. Be judicious in deciding the job you should do yourself. Try to delegate as much as possible.
- Be precise and clear in your communication, be it verbal or written. Instructions to your subordinates should be very clear otherwise at the end of the day everybody's efforts may go waste.
- Keep your table tidy and encourage everyone to do the same. The papers and files should be well-arranged. This saves a lot of time.
- Be brief and business-like while meeting visitors. Those who unnecessarily prolong discussions, should be firmly told not to do so. Avoid offering tea or coffee to visitors and if it has to be offered, make sure that it is served in least possible time.
- Advise important visitors to seek prior appointment as far as possible. The same practice should be followed when you go to meet somebody.
- Plan your tours wisely and try to cover as many assignments as are conveniently possible in one visit. Keep addresses and telephone numbers properly recorded in your diary and it should be readily available.

- Attend promptly to small matters like submitting TA Bills, verifying your GPF account, sending replies to various letters which cannot be passed on to the office, etc. A reminder will only add to your work. You are likely to take more time in recollecting the facts once reply is delayed.
- If you attend a meeting, try to find out when your presence is required and be present accordingly. In case it is not possible to do so, take some paper or file which may be gone through, if your participation in the meeting is not required for some length of time.
- Last, believe that others' time is as important as that of yours. Never waste others' time due to your lack of planning. Ultimately, it is the output of the whole organisation which matters and not merely yours.

These are some of the principles which should be followed in order to make best use of Business Time. The list is not exhaustive and many more points can be added.

Social Time

Social Time is the time you give to your own development, to your family and friends and for social activities. Many businessmen and executives feel that their business obligations are so heavy that they cannot find sufficient time for their family. Their thinking is totally wrong and counter-productive. Such people end up by paying a heavy price for their so-called busy schedule. Proper management of social time is as important as the other two aspects of time. Some important aspects of Social Time Management are:

- All family members should meet at least once, every day, and exchange information and views. This promotes close family bonds and lays the foundation for a happy and successful life.
- At least one morning in a week should also be reserved for the family. And, once or twice a year, all should go out of town for a brief holiday.
- Some people develop a habit of carrying office files to their residence. As far as possible, this should be avoided.

- Social visits and parties are unavoidable, but too much of them can destroy your private life. So carefully choose the occasions, which should be attended. You should also develop the art of saying 'no', if you find it difficult to attend some occasion. Writing a good letter or giving a courteous phone call is the most practical way of doing so.
- For every visit, lay down an average time-limit. Once people come to know that you do not waste any time, and even when you visit them you spend only half an hour or an hour utmost, they will respect your sense of time.
- Social visits should be preceded by some intimation. Unscheduled visits always take a long time than pre-planned ones.
- You must have some time for daily thinking. The greater is your responsibility, the more time you need for thinking. Early morning walks can be a good time to think. This time should not at all be wasted in gossiping.
- Waiting at places like airport, railway or bus station can be used for thinking or reading. Travelling also provides an excellent opportunity for thinking and reading.
- Reading is an important aspect of social time. If you analyse your reading material, you will find that it falls into the following categories:

    (a) Daily newspapers, magazines on current affairs;

    (b) Professional magazines;

    (c) Professional books;

    (d) General books and

    (e) Classics

The first principle is to be selective in your reading; and second to plan your reading. For instance, do not buy 15 or 20 magazines. Select the essential ones and go through them properly. As regards books, you should make a realistic list of books to be read every year. Such a list should also provide a margin for any new book which should be read immediately. Some portion of reading time should be reserved for professional magazines and latest books in your subject so that you are always up-to-date in your line of work.

Reading the daily newspaper is not only a habit but also a necessity. However, one should be selective here also. There is no point in going through too many newspapers. The choice should be limited to two or three papers. One should also develop the habit of reading them rapidly and meaningfully.

- Apart from these personal needs, one should find some time for social activity also. This will depend upon the individual's liking. But it should be carefully selected and the contribution should be meaningful. It should not be merely for the sake of it, otherwise, it may turn out to be counter-productive. One can serve the society through such activities and derive satisfaction. A well-planned man can easily find time for such activities also.

It may not be possible to follow all these above-mentioned aspects of time management at once, but as one proceeds in this direction, they will automatically be followed. And then, you will have time for every necessary activity.

Motivate Your Subordinates

In any organisation, of all the resources, man is the most important resource. The progress and success of an organisation depends mainly upon its human resource. Therefore, managing this resource well becomes very important. Unless your subordinates feel motivated, no amount of hard work or knowledge at your level will be able to achieve the desired results. It is, therefore, essential to keep your people properly motivated. We always pay more attention towards resources like building, equipments, furniture, etc. At times, the bosses are unduly concerned about working hours also. It is not that these things are not important. They certainly are, but in my view, these are subservient to man itself, who is the core of the organisation. Unless there is an inner urge to work, no amount of external facilities can motivate a person to improve his productivity. They can at best extend marginal help.

Before we come to some practical tips on the subject, I must make it clear that inner urge is something which is always present in a human being. Everyone wants to work sincerely and derive pleasure out of it. In some, this urge may be dormant and it is a question of bringing this urge out. Human beings are basically good and this fact is to be accepted before making efforts in motivating them. The approach should, therefore, be to trust your people. Someone may say, trusting may at times be harmful. To this I will only say that non-trusting will always be harmful while trusting may be so only occasionally. By trusting each other, the organisation always stands to gain. Of course, trusting does not at all mean not being careful, that one has always to be. Even while walking on the road one has to be careful. This does not mean that one should not walk on the road.

It should also be remembered that trusting is a two-way process, but initiative has to come from those in superior positions. My experience is that the same set of people give excellent output, once an atmosphere of trust is created in the organisation. The general impression that these days people don't work is not correct. Here are some important tips for motivating your subordinates:

- The pre-condition of motivation is the realisation of common objective. The goal of the organisation should be well-defined and it should be known to everyone including the lower level employees.
- Every individual should know his role in the realisation of the goal and feel proud of it. A feeling should be created in the organisation that everyone is important at his place and should be dealt with dignity. The dignity of the lowest paid employee is as important as that of the Chief Executive or perhaps even more than him.
- The experience is that more than 80 per cent of the employees respond positively when approached with an open and honest mind. Others may not. But before arriving at any conclusion, they should be given the benefit of doubt. You should think from their point of view. Maybe, their past experiences have not been good or their personal lives have not been happy or maybe, some injustices have been done to them in personal matters. If these facts are taken care of, another 10 per cent will follow suit and will fall in the mainstream of the organisation.
- The remaining 10 per cent or less may be the trouble-making elements. We need not be unduly concerned about them. The only factor which should be kept in mind when dealing with them is an open approach. You should be careful of not getting biased towards them and deal with them on merits. This includes firm action whenever necessary. The experience is that such occasions rarely arise. The force of 90 per cent is enough to keep them dormant.
- Communication is something very important for maintaining motivation in the organisation. In the absence of proper

communication even good intention of the management or employees is misunderstood and leads to unhealthy situation.

- It is necessary to create forums where communication may take place in healthy atmosphere. This may be in the form of joint councils, quality circles, periodical meetings, etc. National festivals provide a good opportunity to communicate with your subordinates in an informal atmosphere.
- There should be minimum secrecy about decisions. Once we accept the principle of participative management, I do not see any reason why should any decision be secret. It may be so in rare cases. The fact is that greater is the secrecy in the organisation, greater are the chances of conflict.
- The service/personnel matters of the subordinates should be taken care of in time, otherwise they take the shape of grievances. Matters like annual increment, EB crossing, sanction of GPF advance, leave sanction, TA bill sanction, etc., which appear small and routine, are very important from the point of view of an individual. Such matters should be attended to expeditiously. I have come across several cases where there have been criminal neglect in the disposal of such matters. No wonder, the affected employees had lost all their initiatives.
- Another important factor is the working condition. It should be ensured that the working conditions are reasonably good within the financial constraints of the organisation. I am of the view that lavish expenditure is not necessary for this. All that is needed is to take timely care of the furniture and other equipments and little change of habits. It is not fair to expect good work from a person who sits on a broken chair. Also, unnecessary expenditure should not be incurred for senior officers, and there should only be a reasonable gap between the working conditions of the officers and the staff.
- There should be regular effort to keep the employees as up-to-date in their knowledge as far as possible. The senior officers get several opportunities of interaction with the outer

world and thus remain updated in their knowledge. The staff does not get such opportunities. While equal opportunity may not be possible, their knowledge should be updated through training, seminars or other forms of discussion. My experience in this regard has been very positive. Most of the staff respond very well, if the job is done seriously.

In the end, it should be noted that the success of all the above steps depends upon your transparent sincerity and integrity. If it is not there, no technique can succeed. Therefore, it is essential that you act as a living example to them. Then only all these tips will work and everyone in the organisation will enjoy working with lot of satisfaction and happiness.

Plan Your Meetings

In today's work culture, a lot of time is spent in meetings. Therefore, if meetings are not planned or conducted properly their effectiveness is lost. Nowadays, there is a tendency to call a meeting for every small matter and sometime it is an excuse for inaction. Someone has rightly said, "Meeting is a gathering of gentlemen who singly do nothing and collectively decide that nothing can be done." It is also said, "Meeting is a process in which hours are converted into minutes." While these are some of the cynical remarks about the meetings, they give us a definite message and the message is that meetings may be a waste of time, if not conducted properly. A manager has to conduct a large number of meetings involving several departments. The subjects also relate to various activities, regulatory as well as developmental. Therefore, the proper conduct of the meeting and the follow-up action becomes very important. Here are some tips on how to plan and conduct a meeting in an effective manner:

- First of all, the objective of calling a meeting should be very clear and its agenda should be drawn accordingly.
- The list of participants should be carefully prepared, as inviting unnecessary persons may be counter-productive. The level of participation should also be kept in mind. It should be ensured that those who participate are in a position to take decisions or are in a position to effectively communicate with the decision-makers in their departments.
- The date, time and venue of the meeting should be carefully chosen. There should be sufficient notice unless it is an emergency meeting. If the participants are senior officers

from the other departments, their convenience should also be kept in view.
- The place should be such which may accommodate the participants comfortably. It should be ensured that there are enough chairs and there is no confusion in the seating arrangement. Everyone should know his place so that there is no interchange of places during the course of meeting.
- The meeting should be properly structured. If all the participants are not required throughout, they should not be expected to remain present throughout the meeting. In fact, different timings can be given to different officers in structured meetings. This increases the efficacy of the meeting and senior officers from all the departments will also express their keenness to attend the meeting themselves.
- The officers may be allowed to leave after their subject has been discussed and their presence throughout should not be insisted/expected.
- If the meeting is a periodic one, last meeting's minutes should be considered first and the action taken thereon should be reviewed. There should be no compromise on the assurance given by the officers in the previous meeting unless there are compelling reasons.
- If the meeting is not a periodic one, the purpose of calling a meeting and the points of consideration should be briefly and effectively put forward by the chairperson.
- The environment of the meeting should be such that every participant feels free to give his opinion. At the same time, a sense of business should prevail throughout. It does not mean that there should not be any humorous remark. In fact, such occasional remarks add to the effectiveness of the meeting by making the environment a little informal.
- The duration of the meeting is very important. It depends upon the purpose of the meeting. It should neither be conducted hurriedly nor very leisurely. If more information is required for taking decisions or matters require further discussion, the meeting should be postponed.

Plan Your Meetings

- The notes of the meeting should be taken down by a responsible person and the minutes should be prepared at the earliest possible. Quick despatch of minutes is of great help in making the meeting effective. The minutes should neither be very brief nor unnecessarily large. They should convey the message/decision effectively, and there should be least possibility of misinterpretation. Ambiguity should be avoided in regard to the person or the department responsible for compliance.
- A time-limit should be set for compliance of the decisions. In case it cannot be met, the concerned person or department should communicate at the earliest giving reasons therefore.
- Tea, snacks or meals should be served depending upon the duration and timings of the meeting in such a way that there is least disturbance and wastage of time. Instructions in this regard should be given in advance, and there should be no last minute confusion.
- When the participants are from outside, the arrangement for their reception, entry, name-plates, etc., should be made in advance so that there is no inconvenience caused to them.
- In case of periodic meetings, the date should generally be a fixed one so that all the participants plan their activities accordingly. Only in rare cases, the date should be changed. If so, sufficient notice should be given.
- At times it may not be possible for some officers to attend the meeting and they may send their representatives in the meeting. So long it is done in good faith, it should be accepted unless the presence of a certain official is essential. In that case, the alternative course of action should be explored.
- It should be remembered that the meetings are not attended well when the participants feel that their presence is not required or their time is likely to be wasted. It may be so because no decisions are taken in the meetings. These factors are to be taken care of.
- Quite often the opinion expressed in the meeting is reversed when the proposal is processed on file. This tendency is not

correct. It shows that opinion was not expressed freely. Also, if this is done for the purpose of showing importance, it should be dealt with sternly and such tendencies should be curbed.

- In the end, it should be remembered that meetings are very good means of taking decisions correctly and quickly. In addition, they also provide a good opportunity of interaction between various officers. Many opinions which cannot be expressed on files or through formal channels can be expressed in the meetings and the decisions can be taken with collective wisdom. But it depends upon how effectively the meeting is conducted, otherwise it may be a disaster too.

Dealing with Official Documents

Dealing with official documents is one of the most important aspects of management in all offices and more so in those which deal with public. In fact, the whole process of decision-making starts with the receipt of a letter or petition. It is, therefore, absolutely essential that all the letters received in the office should be dealt with effectively right from the beginning. Unfortunately, there is a tendency of taking letters in a very casual manner which results in delay and at times 'no action' at all. No wonder, the image of administration or management goes down and confidence of public has been lost. Today, even an important citizen cannot be sure of appropriate timely action on his application, what to say of a commoner. No doubt, the quantum of papers has increased immensely but so have the tools and aids available for their disposal. It is, therefore, incorrect to say that ineffective disposal is for lack of resources. It may be so in some cases, but it is more due to lack of seriousness and systems. In this chapter, I shall discuss certain steps which should be taken for the effective disposal of documents. The steps suggested are more applicable to the public offices but the principles, in general, apply to all offices.

A public office receives papers from various sources. While each of them is important, the image of the office is formed on the basis of the disposal of dak received from the public. Here are some important tips for effective dealing of the *dak*:

- Marking of *dak* should be considered to be a very important activity and not a routine one. A responsible officer or official should be entrusted the job of marking. His duty should be only to mark the department or officer on the papers and not to write any order or instruction. However, if the volume of documents is much, he may be advised to segregate it into two different categories: those requiring close attention and those requiring not so close attention. In addition, documents requiring immediate attention may be kept separate and put up personally, if necessary.

- The documents requiring close attention should never be signed in a hurry. The time should be earmarked when you are undisturbed for this purpose. It is always better to spend more time at this stage than to look into it when it is reported on file. It ultimately saves time.
- The orders passed on the *dak* are very important and should not be taken in a routine manner, e.g., asking for report on every letter may not be necessary. If done so, it may reduce the seriousness of asking for a report. On the other hand, all such *dak* in which report is asked for, should be recorded separately so that proper monitoring may be done periodically.
- The orders passed on the documents should be clear and without any ambiguity. This will expedite the disposal and the subordinates will process it in a positive manner.
- Documents requiring not so close attention may be signed by some other responsible officer. However, if workload can be managed, it is always better to mark at Head of Department level. In case no report is asked for, the instructions should be such that the subordinate officers feel responsible and deal with it effectively. The order should reflect the trust in the subordinate officers and at the same time a sense of business.
- Very important documents should be sent along with a covering note and the office copy of the notes should be saved in folders as hard or soft copies. Separate folders may be kept for all the officers working under you. Whenever any of these officers visit your office, there should be instructions for him to see his folder and take note of the pending references.

- Anonymous letters/complaints, etc., should generally be discouraged. If such letters come from the higher authority, they should be disposed of immediately with a brief reply, if asked for. This will curb the tendency greatly and will generate confidence in your officers and staff.
- There are certain matters which are repeatedly brought to the notice of the head of the office and particularly so when there is change of an officer. While such letters should be dealt with an open mind, undue suspicion towards previous officers may be counter-productive.
- Important letters should be acknowledged and this should be done responsibly. Also, as far as possible, an action taken on the petition should be communicated to the applicant unless considered otherwise from an administrative point of view. This will develop confidence in the public and reminders or repeated applications will not be received.
- Reminders should be taken very seriously. Reminders help no one. They increase the work at every level and also indicate the inefficiency of the office. While some reminders may be received because of overlapping, most of them are the result of non-communication or delay in disposal. The Head of Department should take the responsibility himself and develop a culture where the reminder is looked upon with contempt. In one of my assignments, a motto, 'Reminder is Shame', was coined and a call was given to make the office a 'Zero Reminder Office'. This was infused at every level in such a way that there was healthy competition in disposing the receipts as early as possible, and the office became almost a zero reminder office within a short period.
- It may also be remembered that ultimately it is the person behind the document, which matters and not the document. The objective should be to give satisfaction to the person behind and not the disposal of the document. A firm 'no' at times gives more satisfaction than no action. The person in that case has other avenues to explore.

- It should also be kept in mind that the rules are only the guidelines and they should be interpreted in such a way that human aspects are not lost. This attitude also helps in quick disposal of matters.
- Aids like photocopier, fax machine, computer, telephone, etc., should be effectively used for quick disposal of documents. Many times an important reference can be disposed of then and there, if we take the help of these facilities.
- My experience is that quick and effective disposal of documents is a great instrument in achieving your objectives. It discourages those who exploit the lethargy of the system and also those who exploit the common man in the name of the system.
- Attentiveness towards the documents received in the office keeps you informed of the happenings in your area and adds to your strength and effectiveness. Therefore, it is worthwhile to spend little more time in going through them. This is also a great help in stress-free management.

Effective Touring

Touring is an essential and important part of administration. Certain amount of touring has been prescribed for all levels of officers, particularly in District Administration. A close monitoring of these tours is supposed to be carried out at Government level. However, with increasing workload and uncertainties of multifarious duties, the greatest casualty has been touring. While there is need of reviewing the norms of touring in the changed circumstances, its importance can never be undermined. In fact, in public administration or related sector, there is no substitute to touring. However, there is need of making the touring more effective keeping in view the constraints of time, money, etc. My personal experience is that an effective tour is more productive and meaningful than sitting in the office whole day with all sincerity. In addition, it is refreshing and makes you feel more energetic and confident. The facts which come to notice during touring, remain in memory for a longer period and many problems are automatically solved while the officer is on tour without his or her passing any instructions. Here are some tips for effective touring:

- First of all, the importance of touring should be accepted. Unless a tour is undertaken with conviction, it can never be effective.
- Believe that there are enough resources for touring. Lack of time or funds can never be the constraints, if we plan our tour properly.
- It is necessary to plan the tour properly as it saves your time in so many other areas. An officer who plans well for his tours, can keep everyone alert and in confidence. The public

or customers can be faced with much more conviction and confidence if you know the field conditions personally.

- Tours can be divided into two categories: (i) Regular tours and (ii) Contingency tours. My advice is that regular tours should be undertaken throughout the year even if there are no instructions from the above. It is all the more necessary in the present days as the scope of public administration or consumer needs have grown very vast. The contingency tours should be undertaken promptly whenever the situation so requires.
- The regular tour days should be fixed in advance and, if possible, tours should be undertaken during those days only. As District Magistrate and later as Commissioner, I had fixed about two days every week for touring. No Court work was fixed for those days and the tour programme was made known to everyone. As a result, there was no complaint about my non-availability at the Headquarters. Only in extraordinary circumstances, the touring was dropped or changed. This proved very effective and the work became stress-free.
- Regular touring should be undertaken with prior intimation and, if possible, the details of the matters to be looked into should be sent in advance. I had a practice of maintaining a file of each Tehsil and Block in which every important pending matter was noted. The very fact that the subordinates knew that such files were with me, action on them was automatically taken.
- The sole purpose of touring should not be to reprimand your subordinates but it should be mainly to guide them and to appreciate their problems, if any. Quite often the situation is found to be different than what you feel about it sitting at the Headquarters.
- The subordinate staff should be made to feel at ease during tour otherwise the purpose is not fully achieved. However, a sense of business should prevail throughout.

Effective Touring

- You should ensure that officers and staff accompanying you during the touring are taken due care of. They should neither be neglected nor pampered. It is useful at times to find out about their arrangements, conveniences, etc.
- One of the important points during touring, particularly for administrative officers, is the hospitality or the arrangements made by the official staff for the benefit of the visitor. One should normally be guided by convention. While one should not be very fussy about small things, a lavish hospitality should de discouraged and at times emphatically refused. This sends very positive signals about you. Obviously, you should mean it and should not do it merely for the sake of publicity. I have come across officers who pretend to like simple food while expecting a lavish one in their heart. You should make a reasonable payment without giving undue importance to it. At the same time you should not forget to express your sincere appreciation for the efforts made by the staff.
- While touring your steno should always accompany you and, as far as possible, orders should be passed on the spot. A brief tour-note should be prepared during all regular tours and be kept in record.
- While deciding the place of night stay during the tour, the available facilities and the convenience of your staff should also be taken into consideration. Sometimes more energy of the staff goes away in arranging for the tour than attending their official work. This should be avoided and discrimination should be shown in this regard.
- These days there is constraint of budget for travelling. Therefore, it is essential that full utilisation of the tours should be made. While going to distant places, effort should be to cover more areas and, if necessary, the duration of tour be extended.
- It is also important to note that it is not necessary to undertake all tours yourselves. All the officers should be encouraged

to undertake effective touring and it should be properly monitored.
- The frequency of the touring should be decided in such a way that its effectiveness is maintained.
- The public representatives, public, customers, press, bar, etc. should be properly informed about your tours and should be encouraged to meet you during touring. It should be ensured that you are accessible during your tours to the common man and unnecessary time is not lost in your personal care.
- It should be remembered that if you undertake tours effectively many of the false visitors and petitions will stop coming to you and the common man will feel more confident about the system or your organisation. This, on one hand, reduces the demand on your office time while you are at the headquarters and, on the other hand, puts you in a position to deal with the problems in much more effective and realistic manner.

Appraising Subordinates

All departmental heads have to write ACRs (Annual Confidential Reports or Remarks) of their subordinates at the end of the year. This is one of the most important functions and has to be carried out responsibly. In fact, writing of ACRs plays an important role in the performance and motivation of the subordinates. There should be a feeling among them that the ACRs will be written with an open mind and trivial incidents shall not be taken into account. Some officers are known for giving adverse remarks and such an impression creates unhealthy environment in the organisation. One should, therefore, be very objective while writing ACRs. Moreover, motivated adverse remarks become difficult to justify when representations are received and ultimately, it tells upon the integrity of the officer himself.

In order to develop an objective approach in writing ACRs, it is necessary to understand certain basics about the system of writing ACRs. These are as follows:

- The writing of ACR is a system of appraisal, the purpose of which is to evaluate personal performance in the background of the objectives set for the organisation. Therefore, the objectives of the organisation are very important and any observation not connected with the organisation's objectives need not be made.
- Further, the objective of performance appraisal is not to find faults but to develop the person in order to make him perform better. This implies that:
    (a) his role in developing a sense of accountability for achieving job objective should be clarified;

(b) only his current job performance should be examined and assessed;
(c) he should be motivated to improve his performance;
(d) his weakness or lack of experience which may require further training or guidance should be identified;
(e) he should be encouraged to improve in his present job and for promotion;
(f) he should develop a sense of satisfaction or fear for non-achievement.

Appraisal should be undertaken with these objectives in mind.

- The periodicity of the appraisal has to be kept in view. Small matters can be pointed out in periodic review which will be in the form of monthly staff meetings, monthly statements, etc. At times verbal or written, warning may also be issued. However, these should not unnecessarily be made ground for giving adverse comments, if the purpose of issuing such warnings is already served. Only on consistent failure to mend, the adverse remarks have to be given. Also in periodic reviews, appreciation should be expressed whenever it is called for.

- It is important to have certain parameters of appraisal to make the appraisal more objective. While these parameters may vary from job to job, some general parameters are always valid. These are (a) General Performance, (b) Job Knowledge, (c) Work Output, (d) Work Quality, (e) Decision-making, (f) Commitment, (g) Relationship with others, (h) Reliability, (i) Adaptability and (j) Integrity.

All these parameters are clear in themselves and more can be added, if applicable to a particular job.

- As mentioned earlier, the purpose of writing ACR is not to find fault or to condemn. Therefore, areas, which need improvement, should be pointed out in a suitable manner without making any adverse comments. Such observations should include steps to be taken for such improvement. If the appraisee is considered fit for promotion, it should be said so and if not, steps to make up the deficiency should be mentioned.

- While commenting on the integrity of a person, one needs to be very careful as it is a sensitive issue. If there is only suspicion about the integrity of an appraisee, it should not be made the sole basis of withholding it. Tendency to give non-committal remarks about the integrity, even if there is no ground for doing so, should also be avoided. If the integrity is beyond doubt, it should be so stated. If it is doubtful and further verification is required, it may be asked for. Needless to say, that there should always be a good faith.

- 'Adverse Remarks' is an area where one has to be very careful. Though there are no set rules, but adverse remarks should be given as a last resort and at the same time one should not hesitate to do so, if it is really called for. However, the basis of such remarks should be very clear and as far as possible in a documentary form. If it is so, it would not be difficult to deal with the representation received from the appraisee subsequently. Sometimes an adverse remark has its purpose and one need not be very rigid if the purpose is served, and in that case, there is no harm in recommending erasion or modification of such remarks.

- At the end of the ACR, an overall grade has to be given. Generally five grades are there, namely excellent or outstanding, very good, good, fair and poor. A normal distribution among these five categories is approximately 5 per cent, 20 per cent, 60 per cent, 10 per cent, 5 per cent. There may be exceptions, but any wild deviation is a matter of careful study.

In the end, it has to be noted once again that the ultimate purpose of appraisal is building of the organisation through individuals. If that purpose is not served, appraisal in itself has no meaning. Therefore, one should display full integrity while writing the ACRs of one's subordinates.

Efficient Use of the Telephone

When I joined service, telephonic network was very poor except in big towns. I distinctly remember that in 1980, when I was Deputy Secretary in the Industries Department at Lucknow, it was so difficult to contact even Kanpur. Whenever such need arose, it was a job in itself and, if I could succeed within a reasonable time, I felt elated. Things have greatly changed since then and today telephone has become the quickest and most easily accessible mean of communication. Naturally, it had its impact on the functioning of administration. With the advent of PCO/STD booths as well as mobile phones, almost every common man has access to telephone. While the number of calls received by an officer in earlier days were limited, today they have gone up manifold. Also, the kind of filtering which was done earlier by the personal staff is neither possible nor desirable today. It is more so, when one occupies a position which deals with public. As a result, quite a good amount of an officer's time is spent on conversation over telephone both at office as well as at home. This time has to be managed effectively as well as efficiently. Not all are able to do. As a result, at times a telephone call becomes a nuisance and defeats the very purpose of having a telephone. Not only this, often owing to undesirable responses the official as well as personal lives of the employees may get adversely affected. One, therefore, needs to be very vigilant while attending a telephone. Following tips in this regard may be helpful.

- I would like to impress that when one holds an important position, many of us forget that a certain price has to be paid for that. One such price is in the form of attending too many telephone calls, some of them at odd hours. If one takes it as an indication of one's importance and a matter of privilege, the dilemma disappears to a great extent.

- One should also remember that the importance of telephone ringing is realised only when it does not ring. One only needs to interact with a retired officer or an officer occupying a less important position to know how eagerly they look forward to receive a phone call. When nobody rings up, then only one realises the importance of a telephone call.

- In order to avoid unnecessary calls at home, one should reach office in time. Then only is it morally right to refuse receiving a call at home to the members or the representatives of the public. This tendency is then curbed on its own, if people know that you reach office in time.

- At office, the personal staff should also come in time and be available for receiving calls. It should be ensured that he is courteous and efficient in handling the calls. At the outset he should give his introduction so that time is not wasted in initial enquiries. His attitude should always be helpful and he should give correct position on the query unless it is necessary to do otherwise in larger interest. That too should be done only occasionally. If there are instructions for not passing on the calls on account of some important meeting or other matter, he should tell the caller about the time when he or she should ring up.

- If the call has to be passed on to you, he should do so promptly and you too should do the same. Some officers have the habit of letting the buzzer sound unnecessarily before picking up the phone. Often they do so to show their importance. This helps no one including you yourself. In the process, your time is equally wasted. For the caller it is not only waste of time but of money too.

- An important point of contention is who should come on the phone first. At times, this may be funny as well as embarrassing. This situation is further complicated by the personal staff, if he is not mature enough. Unnecessary fussiness on this count should be avoided. There is no harm, if you come on the phone first even if the caller or the called person is junior to you. In all probability, doing so enhances your prestige and earns you more respect.

- The conversation over telephone should be brief and effective. This is necessary for many reasons. First, time is important and should not be wasted in meaningless conversation. Second, there is an opportunity cost to it. The time saved may be used for better purpose. Third, if it is a STD call, money is also important. Last, by keeping the phone unnecessarily busy, you may be missing an important call or may be giving a wrong message to others.
- Certain dignity in your conversation over phone, particularly in office, is a must. At times, you may be in the company of others, who watch your language, style, body language and the contents. By being decent and business-like, you give a good message to them too.
- While talking over telephone, a suitable piece of paper and a pen should be readily available to you. In most of the cases something has to be written down. If it can be done without any loss of time, it is for everybody's advantage. Some officers have a tendency to note down the message on the cover of a file or on some other important documents. In that case, there are good chances of it getting lost causing unnecessary inconvenience and embarrassment. Therefore, messages should be noted at one place and attended to promptly.
- Never make a promise over telephone which you don't intend to keep or are not in a position to do so. Words should be carefully used while responding to the request of the caller. You should not only be cautious, but also truthful in your words. This helps in the long run even if you sound cool in the short run. Your credibility is established over a period of time and people mostly go by that than by your immediate words.
- Never think that the matter gets finished by your decent response over the telephone. One call out of many may not be important for you but for the caller it is very different. He

Efficient Use of the Telephone

will remember every word you uttered and will expect you to act on them. Therefore, prompt and suitable action on what you say is a must. A suitable system to do so should be devised in order to avoid future embarrassment or loss of credibility.

- At times, the calls are made for seeking an appointment. Sometimes it may be offending also. In that case, there is no point in showing undue displeasure and the appointment should be given without any fuss, if you are in a position to do so.
- Callers are also in the habit of asking you as to when could they contact you again. It is mostly difficult to give a definite time-frame particularly when you yourself are unaware of the status of his or her petition. Such requests should not be taken very seriously and it can generally be handled by general answers like 'after a week or so', 'please find out later', or 'let me first look into the matter'. However, if it is possible to give a definite time-frame, it should be given. It is also sometimes useful to note down the contact number of the caller so that he or she may be informed over telephone either by you or someone instructed by you. My experience is that this gesture is very useful and rewarding.
- You should not allow the caller to take unnecessary liberty with you. With experience you should be in a position to judge this. It often happens when the caller is in the company of others on whose behalf he is making a call. To some extent he can be given the benefit of doubt or ignored, but beyond a point, he should be firmly told to talk sense and to be brief.
- A helpful tip is to recognise the fact that a meaningful dialogue over telephone is helpful to all. Were the caller to meet you personally, he would have in all probability taken more time and in the process, wasted yours as well as his

time. In fact, you should encourage disposal over telephone. I encourage visitors to give their phone numbers on the petition that they can be contacted over telephone, if needed. This has been found very useful.

- Even anonymous calls should not be totally ignored. There can be some substance in them too. If so, it should be picked up and utilised in the larger interest.
- At times, the caller does not want to disclose his or her identity to your staff. When faced with such a situation, it is wise to receive the call and to deal with it as the situation demands.
- When you are engaged in an important meeting or discussion, it is better to tell the personal staff not to pass on the calls. By doing so, you do justice to both. However, the message given to the caller by the personal staff should be very clear. Also, the details of all the calls received during that period should be placed before you at the earliest so that you may call back those whom you consider necessary.
- You should also cultivate the habit of making some calls personally. This helps in many ways. Your personal staff comes to know that you are not always dependent on them. At times, there may be some useful feedback about the behaviour of your personal staff in your absence or even in presence. This feedback can be used at an appropriate time. Personal calling also leaves a very positive impact on the person called upon. Last, if it is an STD call, office money is also saved. It is also easy to give suitable instructions, if the person called upon is not available.
- Dealing with telephone calls at home is a more difficult proposition. If not done with wisdom, it may also become a source of disharmony in the family, particularly between you and your wife, who may be already upset by your long office hours.

- As a rule, official calls at home should be avoided unless your residence is also your camp office. It is more so, if you pay full attention to your office and are available there for sufficient time. However, some room for emergency or the ignorance of the caller should always be left and you should not get annoyed, if someone calls you at home for official purpose.
- An important point to decide is as to who should receive the call at home, if it is not a camp office. Opinions may vary on this. Some may like to keep a peon or even instruct the domestic servant to receive the calls, others may prefer to do so themselves. Both have merits and demerits. However, given the fact that the peon or the domestic servant is generally an illiterate or semi-literate person and is not in a position to respond intelligently, the gain may be more than loss by the confusion he may create by his mishandling. The biggest victim will be your close friends and relatives who may stop calling you because of this. I, therefore, feel that overall it is better to receive the call yourself (including your spouse) even if it is inconvenient at times.
- It is also a myth that time is saved, if you don't receive the call yourself. In fact, it may be the other way round. Generally, the moment the telephone starts ringing, one's attention is drawn towards it and till one knows about the caller, one may not be in a position to attend to anything else. I was surprised to see that the Police Commissioner Hyderabad, who was my friend and with whom I was staying during my election duty as an observer, used to receive every phone call himself. He told me that overall it was more convenient for him and I agreed with him.
- Once people know that it is you or your wife who receives the call, most of them are careful while making a call at home. Still there will be many offenders known or unknown, who may not care for your inconvenience. They

are the most difficult lot and should be handled with care. In no case, the temper should be lost. For in that way, it is only you who pay the price. The best prescription is that either let the caller prevail upon you or you prevail upon him. It will depend upon the situation and the decision has to be taken by using your wisdom and experience.

- Last, the role of your spouse is very important in the handling of calls at home. In fact, she may be the worst victim of your importance or popularity. The greatest wisdom lies in dealing with her. She suffers on two counts. One, the little time she gets with you is stolen by the telephone and second, if she receives the call, she may not be welcome and be simply asked to pass on the phone to her husband. She has to be lovingly told that it is the price which she has to pay for marrying you. Most of the time it works.

Organising a Conference

These days it is very common to organise seminars, workshops and conferences. They not only provide a good forum for updating the knowledge but also a good platform for interaction amongst the participants. Such occasions are also good breathers for those who have a busy schedule and find no time for generating new ideas. To those whose vision becomes narrow on account of constantly being engaged in routine work, these are occasions for taking a broader view of things. Overall, I find them worth the pain and money involved in their organisation. There is no doubt that organisation of such an event is an extra load on the office and its head, but the usefulness and satisfaction derived from its success is far in excess of the load. In short, the gain is always more than the pain.

Despite the above fact, not many managers take the pain to organise such an event either occasionally or periodically. They do so only when such an event is either thrust upon them by tradition or by the superiors. My experience tells me that even when such an event is organised as a result of compulsion, the success of it creates a natural urge for periodical organisation of such events even among the subordinate staff. They look to such an event as an opportunity to show their talent and also feel important in interacting with many either within the organisation or from outside. In any case, such an event cannot be successfully organised without the willing support of the office. Such a climate may have to be created in the beginning by the initiative of the head of the department (HOD). Once the process is set in motion, things move on their own and success becomes natural.

I have had the opportunity of organising such events in a large number. They have been on various subjects at different places and in different styles. All of them have been successful and I can hardly recall any embarrassment. I am, therefore, sharing some basic principles of organising a conference in brief. For the purpose of convenience, I am calling such an event as conference, though the same holds good for events like workshop or seminar. They vary only in style and mode of discussion. As far as organisation is concerned, the principles are almost the same.

- The first step is to develop conviction about the utility of the conference. This is necessary not only in the HOD but also in the second rank managers and ultimately in the entire office. In no case, decision of organising a conference should be taken without taking the second line managers in confidence. Of course, it is impossible to do so without the personal conviction of the HOD.
- Having decided to organise a conference, the HOD should have a brainstorming session with his second line officers. The purpose of the session should be to narrow down the choice of dates, subject, timings and the venue. All these are important for the success of the event. However, there should always be a room for change, at least in the beginning.
- Having broadly decided upon the topic, the dates, the timings and the venue, the HOD should also take into confidence his superiors either formally or informally. If it is not done, the whole affair may collapse, if there are any instructions to the contrary. Such a consultation also helps in getting a better counsel. Many times one may lose sight of certain aspects which are important, and such a consultation may bring them forth.
- After the superiors are taken into confidence, an apex committee should be formed for the organisation of the conference with the HOD as chairman. The constitution of the committee should be broad-based so as to involve all wings of the office. At the same time, it should not be very large. A representative of the Government or the superior

office may also be kept in the committee in order to keep its formal involvement. The coordinator or the member secretary should generally be from the department to which the subject of discussion belongs. If the subject is a general one, then some senior person, who is really interested in this kind of activity, should be made the coordinator.

- The apex committee should meet at the earliest and finalise the topic, dates, venue and the timings. The dates should neither be very near nor be very distant unless they are already fixed. In that case preparations should begin only in reasonably advance time.
- The whole process of organisation should be divided into sub-activities and a sub-committee be formed to look after each of them. This not only makes the participation broad-based, it also lightens the burden of the apex committee. Some examples of sub-committees are finance committee, reception committee, souvenir committee, transport committee, etc. The sub-committees should be asked to prepare their plans at the earliest.
- One most important and essential step is to prepare a tentative budget by the finance committee, which should be discussed in the apex committee and finalised soon. The estimates both on receipt and expenditure sides should be realistic. There should also be enough room for variations, which are quite probable. After the budget is finalised, all efforts should be made to stick to that.
- Minutes of the apex committee meetings as well as those of the sub-committees should be recorded and circulated at the earliest. This is essential to avoid any communication gap and also to ensure accountability.
- Two most important parts of a conference are the opening session and the closing session. The success of the conference largely depends on them. The chief guest for both the occasions should be chosen carefully. The persons chosen for the purpose should not only be prominent but also be interested in the subject. His availability should be reasonably

certain, and if doubtful, it is better to choose a less prominent person. Last minute absence of the chief guest may send wrong signals among the participants and lessen their interest or seriousness.

- Request to the proposed chief guests should be sent in reasonable time and followed by a personal request either directly or through the office. It is also helpful to make a separate request either through the secretary or the minister. Most of the time, such persons are very busy with a great demand on their time. They agree to such an invitation only after judging the importance of the event and the seriousness of the organisation.

- For bringing out the souvenir, the work should begin well in time. Messages from the concerned VIPs should be obtained in time. This requires a proper follow-up which should be entrusted to a smart person and not necessarily a senior person. The documents to be published in the souvenir should be carefully selected. They should not only be relevant to the topic of conference but also make an interesting reading. The objective should be to make the souvenir a collection item. Similarly, the advertisements should also be relevant and optimum in number. The overall mix of the reading and non-reading material should be quite balanced.

- The structure of the proceedings of the conferences should be carefully designed taking into account the nature of the topic, level of the participants, level of the speakers and the objective of the conference. The inaugural and the closing session should be paid particular attention. A well-begun conference is likely to be successful also. Similarly, well-organised closing session is a measure of its success. Both should be short and effective. The timings should be adhered to the extent possible. Long speeches should be avoided except that of the main speaker. Drawing of minute to minute programme and bringing it to the notice of all those sitting on the dais is helpful in this regard.

- The number and kind of persons sitting on the dais should also be carefully decided. At times, it may cause heart-burning among some persons. However, if the objective is kept in mind and a firm approach is adopted, it is not difficult to do so. This number should be optimum, neither too small nor too large.
- The role of media in the success of a conference is very important. Therefore, its proper involvement is a must. A brief press note should be prepared in advance so that the objective and the subject of the conference are clear to them. A press note or an advertisement at appropriate time is also helpful. At the same time, undue publicity should be avoided. A well-organised conference gets good publicity on its own. It should also be remembered that the public at large is not much interested in conference related news. It is mainly the participants and the organisers who pay more attention to such news.
- The selection of venue is very important. It should be well-located and well-known. Even if the expenses are bit higher, it is worthwhile to select a good venue. Good facilities at the place of conference are a must for its success as one single lapse in the arrangement can spoil the whole show.
- The conference should be designed in such a manner that the participants remain interested and alert all the time. Documents to be presented should be short and relevant. There should be ample scope of dialogue wherever permissible. The modern presentation techniques should be made full use of.
- The hospitality part of the conference is important. It should be decent and cost-effective. This also requires some planning. The comforts of the delegates should be ensured at the highest level. They are the most important participants. The menu should be decided carefully. It should be ensured that tea and food are ready in time and there is ample moving space while the same are being served. Some flexibility of timings should also be there as quite often the timings of the

sessions are disturbed due to poor time management or some other reasons.

- Each session of the conference should be reported by a relevant person. The report should be prepared soon after the session and kept ready for presentation in the closing session. The report should be short and effective. Care should be taken to ensure that each speaker gets due coverage. For this, proper facilities should be available at the venue itself. A rough draft of the overall recommendations should also be prepared during the conference only.

- A genuine good attendance in the closing session is the measure of the success of the conference. Effort should be made to have the minister or the secretary of the department as chief guest for the closing session. It helps in the implementation of the recommendations. The deliberations of the conference should be placed before him, objectively covering both appreciation as well as criticism of policies. These are occasions when issues can be put in right perspective without bringing in anything personal about them. Similarly, suggestions should also be placed with an open mind.

- Care should be taken while thanking the participants. No one should be missed, though the message should be brief. A right word of appreciation does wonders and lays the foundation of future successful conferences.

- It is good to organise a separate brainstorming session to finalise the recommendations of the conference soon after its conclusion. They should be properly documented and circulated among all relevant persons. One important thing which should be remembered is that no magic should be expected out of a conference. Yet they serve an important purpose and their benefit is mostly subtle. They are good breathers and mere interaction between the participants is a rare opportunity.

- The credit for success should be shared by all. This is an event which no individual can successfully organise single-handed. The effort is to be made right from the HOD to the lowest person in the office. A suitable word of appreciation or a memento or an award can do wonders for them. Their suggestions for improvements in future should also be obtained before they forget them.

Be Transparent

Our Independence is now more than fifty years old. This period has been very significant in human life. The scientific growth during this period has been so rapid that the management of the society as per its expectation has become a very challenging task. Unfortunately, our work culture and style has not been able to keep pace with the changing needs of the society. This has resulted in great disharmony in almost all areas of interaction both in public as well as private sector. Different graphs look at each other with contempt and without understanding each other's limitations, consider the other as irresponsible. While this feeling may be partly true, it does not lead us to any solution and therefore, the need is to think of necessary changes in the culture and style of administration. This is all the more so in a democratic system where the Government is formed by the representatives of the people themselves.

While the subject of administrative reforms is very vast and voluminous, work has been done and is being done in this area. Here the discussion is confined to a very important aspect which is 'Transparency and Right to Information'. This single reform, if undertaken in right earnest, can take care of many problems one faces in administration today. I can say, without hesitation, that despite so much emphasis on this aspect, the administrative system is still very secretive and often so to its own detriment. It is so partly advertently but mostly inadvertently because of the inherited administrative culture. The British administrative system might have had its own good reasons to maintain undue secrecy in Government decision. It need not be so in a free democratic society where most of the Government activities are welfare-oriented run with public money. The public has full right to know the decisions of the Government, the manner in which they are taken and also the reasons. While this may sound somewhat impractical, the fact is that the public is very appreciative of the situation, if they know the facts and the limitations faced by the decision-makers well. The following example will make this point clearer.

Quite often, the proposals of various departments are not cleared by the finance department for lack of funds. The objections of the finance are often attributed to its negative attitude or lack of understanding of the proposal. Hardly anyone tries to understand its limitation. Even the members of the legislature, who pass the budget, are not aware of the limitations and true implications of budget-making exercises. In one of the big states, the finance secretary got a white paper prepared on the financial position of the state and got it circulated among all those who should know the financial position of the state. It was so much appreciated that many unreasonable or impractical demands were not pressed and decision-making became easier. The information given in the white paper were so elementary that one wondered as to why they were not shared earlier for reasons of secrecy.

The question of transparency and right to information can be looked at from two points of view. One is the legal view which is often talked about these days. The second is to look at it as a matter of expediency. I lay more emphasis on the second. My experience is that when transparency in decision-taking is shown in right earnest and the information is shared in a wise manner, many problems of administration are taken care of, which may be otherwise difficult to handle. It is now well-established that when the information about various development schemes and the funds allocated for them are displayed at a prominent place in the village, the delivery system becomes much better and the level of satisfaction increases substantially. It is also a fact that the issue of corruption in Government is generally exaggerated in the absence of proper data being available to those who label such charges. From this angle, transparency and information-sharing also becomes a tool of defence to those who are victims of the bad reputation of Government machinery.

Now, I come to certain tips which may be helpful in attaining the objectives of transparency and information-sharing. I have applied them in my administrative career and I can say without any reservation that they have never let me down. Of course, one has to be careful and wise while being transparent or sharing information. After all, situations and persons to be dealt with are different and discretion has to be applied from situation to situation and from person to person. However, the general approach has to be the same and secrecy should only be a matter of strategy and not of fear. Here are a few tips.

- The head of the office or a particular department should be accessible within reasonable limits. This fact itself instils great confidence among the members of public. The timings of availability should be well-displayed and it should be ensured that the officers are available during the displayed time. However, in case of urgency, one should be prepared to meet any time.

- The petitions should be received with patience and orders on them be passed carefully. From the viewpoint of the petitioner, this is very important. He should feel that his petition is being paid due attention. When order can be passed then and there, the system of asking for office report or comments should be avoided. I feel it is worth the risk and gives very positive message about the organisation. However, where additional facts are required, a report can be sought but it should be ensured that it is available within reasonable time.

- All petitions should be recorded for the purpose of future references. For this, the use of a computer is very convenient, otherwise a register can also be used. In many cases, the petition has to be handed back to the petitioner for taking it to another officer or department. In doing so, unnecessary hesitation should not be shown. The petitioner will take greater care of the document than you can take. It also saves the time and energy of the office. The only risk is that he may get it photocopied and if subsequently some change in

Be Transparent

the order is required, he may use the photocopy of the previous order, if it suits him. The probability of this is quite low, if due care is taken.

- All information which should be passed on to the public should be passed on in time through suitable media. It may be through notice-board, circulars, newspapers (news or advertisement) or news bulletins. If it is affordable, the organisation should publish a periodic bulletin for sharing information. When done intelligently, it becomes a potent tool for bringing excellence in the organisation.
- Information should be passed on or shared without any bias. Any criticism received as a result thereof should be dealt with in a healthy manner. After all, bona fide mistakes are made only when decisions are taken. Only those who do not take decisions, do not make mistakes. By and large, the system still protects bona fide mistakes. Any exception should be taken as an accident which can happen despite all care.
- Minutes of any meeting should be recorded in the shortest period possible. This not only helps in correct recording but also adds to the credibility of the discussion held in the meeting. Dissenting views, if expressed in good faith, should also be recorded faithfully.
- Petitions received in *dak* should also be processed quickly and in case of delay, an interim reply or acknowledgement should be sent. This saves the office from repeated petitions and also induces confidence in the public.
- The movement of the files should be quick. Any delay, without adequate reason, only adds to the suspicion in those who are affected by such files. In no case, the person behind the file should be made to run parallel to it. It should be stopped firmly.
- The reply to a petition should not be very cryptic. If there are problems in taking a quick or favourable decision, the facts should be mentioned clearly though wisely. If the matter remains open, the same should be conveyed.

- While replying Assembly or Parliament question, undue evasiveness should not be shown. That only leads to trouble subsequently. The hammer should be hit right on the head without caring for the consequences. A frank and correct answer is generally always helpful.
- Public functions and ceremonies should be made use of for sharing information. Many facts, which we consider routine, are important from the viewpoint of the public and the employees. They should be shared at the right time and in adequate measure.
- Field tours are very important for the purpose of transparency and information-sharing. Sitting at the headquarters, it is difficult to appreciate the problems in the field and also the perception they have about the head office. Tours undertaken in light but business-like mood also help the field offices to improve their performance. This greatly takes care of the problems of the public at the local level only.
- Press, TV, Radio and other media are very important and can be effectively used for transparency as well as information-sharing. However, dealings with media should be very objective and business-like. Once the credibility of the organisation is established, informal chats can also be held occasionally.
- When members of the public go to consumer forums, courts or any other channel for the redressal of their grievances, they should still be dealt with in an objective manner. The fact of their going to such forums should not create any adverse opinion while dealing with them or their files. Gradually they find it more expedient to approach you for the redressal of their problems, even if they may get better relief elsewhere. 'Peace and convenience' has its own price and most of them know it well.
- Last, it should always be kept in mind that as a public servant you are custodian of a chair or office and are meant to serve the people. While it is your prerogative to adopt any

approach, the overall goal of public welfare should be uppermost in your mind. The decision taken or the information shared by you is not anything personal. You do so under the authority of the State which derives its power from the people. Therefore, any neglect of their welfare is a challenge to your authority and will turn out to be self-defeating in the ultimate analysis.

Many problems, about which many of us complain today, disappear effortlessly, once an open approach is adopted and we are able to work without stress.

Meeting Visitors

Like telephone, management of visitors is another very important area when you occupy an important position dealing with the public. Your visitors include members of public, representatives of the people, elected members of the state legislature or the Parliament, ex-MLAs and MPs, members of the media and your own staff. They put great demand on your time and attention. The fact is that you exist for them and your access to them is greatly helpful in discharging your duty efficiently and effectively. As a general rule, they should be always welcomed and should know that they are welcome. However, reasonable restrictions may have to be imposed in the larger interest and for optimum utilisation of the time available to you. Though everyone is entitled to develop his or her own plan for managing visitors, certain principles hold true for all.

- First, you should love meeting people. Your importance and existence is only on account of them. If you do not meet them conveniently, eventually you may lose your job and be transferred to a less important post. In any case, the transfer should not be for this reason.
- The feedback you receive from your visitors, be they from any category, is very useful. If received with an open mind, it is a tremendous strength to you which can be used for better command on your job. It also saves you from many misunderstandings and spread of rumours.
- Meeting time should always be planned carefully. It can either be in the forenoon or afternoon. Whatever be the time fixed, you should be available during that period and the

absence should only be exceptional. If possible, your absence should be notified in advance.

- During the fixed time, everyone should be free to meet you. Even if it increases the number of visitors, the pain is worth the gain. Any screening of visitors is likely to create problems. Of course, while meeting visitors you should encourage or direct them to meet at the lower level, if that serves the purpose. A clear message should also go down the line that they should be equally accessible, courteous and helpful. Any default brought to your notice or learnt by other means, should be dealt with firmly.

- Meeting time should be carefully used. During that period there should be direct access to you, preferably at first come first go basis. No time should be wasted between the two visitors. It is always helpful to call in two or three visitors at a time so that after finishing with one, you immediately meet the next. Also, their movement should be so planned that they do not collide with each other.

- The number of chairs placed in front of you during the meeting should be at least two and at the most four. This in itself gives a message to the visitors and in no case should anyone be allowed to gossip or relax. Many visitors have the tendency of showing their importance by trying to sit with you for a longer period, even if there is no purpose. Such visitors should be firmly but courteously told not to do so.

- Visitors should be told to be brief and come directly to the question of the relief sought. The detailed background should be gone through later or when it is absolutely necessary then and there. Also find out, if the petition had been given earlier also and if so, what happened to that. Try to correlate the present petition with the past.

- Encourage visitors to write their contact number, if they have one. This may be very useful, if interim progress is to be reported or additional information is to be sought. This gives importance and confidence to the visitors. Whenever necessary, the contact number should be made use of and the concerned officers or staff should be instructed accordingly. In no case, should it be a mere formality.

- It is helpful to keep an efficient and good steno with you while meeting visitors. Orders which can be passed, should be passed then and there. In doing so, there may be occasional mistakes which can either be rectified or ignored, if brought to your notice later. You should remember the fact that the chances of mistakes in a long drawn decision are no less than that in a quick decision. The system still permits for bona fide mistakes and with your background in mind, there are feeble chances of any finger being raised against you.

- Telephonic instructions down the line should also be given then and there, if required. It gives tremendous satisfaction to the visitors and also makes the lower staff more serious. The steno sitting with you, may be asked to keep follow-up on such instructions.

- One dilemma faced is whether the orders having been passed, should be handed over to the visitors to carry to the concerned level or transmitted through official channel. There is no single answer to it. It depends upon many factors and you are the best judge. I would only say that there is no harm, if it is handed over to the visitor. In all likelihood he will take better care of it and you are also saved from unnecessary follow-up action. The ball is then in his court.

- Many visitors come to you for frivolous matters. It may not be in their interest too. But, when you have fixed some open time, they are entitled to do so and there is no effective mechanism to avoid them. Once they are in, there is no point in showing displeasure or anger. They have, in any case, encroached upon your time. The best thing is to mark their petition to the concerned officer and guide them properly to go to him. It requires less time to do so. Any other approach is likely to take more time and also create unpleasantness. The officers down the line should also be occasionally taken

to task, if most visitors which should go to them, come to you. Such a message should also be spread tactfully.
- Petitions, which require proper follow-up action and involve well-considered decision-making, should be properly recorded and a suitable time-frame be fixed for their disposal. This can be done in various ways. I have experienced that fixing a day in a week for such matters is quite useful. The particular day should be known to the petitioner so that decision may be taken in his presence. In important matters, even the lower staff or officer may be called to present the case before the petitioner.
- The decision taken should be implemented quickly and transparently. A good number of visitors come to you for the follow-up of the decision already taken. If an efficient system of follow-up is developed, you save a lot of time. In that case, the credibility of the organisation also goes up and the number of visitors are further reduced in the process.
- When no relief can be given to the petitioner, he should be clearly, firmly and pleasantly told so. It helps to tell him the reasons also, if they are not to be kept secret for specific reasons. My experience is that a firm quick 'no' gives much better relief to the visitors than to keep his matter hanging. Then he is in a position to go to other forums, if he so decides. The reports sought from such forums should also be sent with an open mind. It should be remembered that we can only try to do justice. Whether justice is really being done or not, is not always in our hands. There may be different perceptions to a similar situation and all may have their own merits.
- Important visitors should be avoided during open hours. Such visitors should be encouraged to seek prior appointment, whenever possible. In case they turn up during open hours, they should be extended due courtesy. It may not be necessary to call them in immediately breaking the queue, but their importance should be recognised in proper manner. It may be either by conveying a message through the peon or the

PA, or by offering a seat elsewhere and even by calling him in and making him to wait for reasonable time. Most of the time your intention will be well-understood and if there is any exception, it should be ignored.

- No tea or coffee should be served during open hours of meeting. At most, it may be offered to the waiting VIP, in which case, it should be ensured that it is served quickly and others are not disturbed.
- Members of the press may also come to you during open hours. Quite often, it is for the purpose of seeking an advertisement. Though such visitors should be discouraged once they are in, they should also be dealt with patiently. The best thing is to mark their request to the concerned officer with suitable instructions, if necessary. Most of the time, such visitors only take chance and have no serious expectations.
- Appointment should be quickly fixed for those who seek it. If it is possible to ward off their request over telephone itself, the same should be encouraged. But if insisted, there should be no undue delay in fixing appointment. A couplet of Kabir as translated below is helpful in this regard.

'What you ought to do tomorrow, do today and what you ought to do today, do now. You never know when your innings may come to an end.'

- Finally, you should remember the advantage of meeting people. In this process, you come across many interesting personalities who may develop into good friends. After all, you are also a human being and need to share your own joys and sorrows. My experience in this regard is very positive.

Organise Your Court Work

*C*ourt work is one of the important constituents of an Officer's work as SDM/SDO, Additional Collector/ADM, Collector/DM and Commissioner. However, there is a growing tendency of taking this work lightly. The easy explanation given is preoccupation in other administrative work. Admittedly the nature of work in these capacities is multifarious and quite often unscheduled duties are to be attended to. It, therefore, becomes difficult to be certain to attend the Court unlike the judicial counterparts.

While there is no denial to this constraint, I am of the view that this constraint itself makes it necessary to organise the court work properly. If there were no such constraints, where was the need of organising? My personal experience has been very positive in this regard and barring once or twice in the whole year, I hardly missed attending the court as SDM, DM and Commissioner. Here are a few important tips to organise your court work:

- Due importance should be accepted for the court work. In fact, it is this work which gives you statutory powers and your importance/effectiveness is due to these powers. Second, it should also be kept in mind that most of the litigants are from the poor sections of society and delay costs them heavily.
- The court days should be chosen carefully. It is better to keep two or three days completely off so that you are fully available for other administrative duties. Touring can also be planned during those days.
- Your court time should also be fixed as far as possible. Full efforts should be made to sit in the court during that time only. Once it is known that you give due importance to court

work, no one will disturb you during your court hours unless there is an extraordinary situation.
- The number of cases fixed for the day should be reasonable taking into account the probable adjournments and it should be in your knowledge. A copy of the cause-list should not only be displayed outside the court, it should be made available to you also right in the morning.
- While you should trust your court staff, you should be the master of your work and not they. It should be ensured that every case is called out and the parties appear before you.
- A flexible approach should be adopted in granting adjournments, etc. It should be based on merits of the case and you should not be fussy about them. This lessens the exploitation of litigants. However, a posture of no-nonsense should always be maintained.
- After hearing the arguments, the judgement should be delivered at the earliest possible. There is a tendency to postpone the judgement repeatedly, particularly, if the case is complicated. This is very detrimental and it is exploited by unscrupulous elements. Only in extraordinary circumstances, should the date fixed for the judgement be changed.
- It should be remembered that quick disposal of cases is in itself a check against filing of unnecessary cases. Quite a number of cases are filed to exploit the delay in the system.

Also remember that your court work is a measure of your judgement, dignity and concern for justice. If court work is dealt with effectively, it goes a long way in making you an effective officer.

Management of Legal Cases

$\mathcal{M}$anagement of court cases is an area of growing importance today. As one goes higher up in the ladder of administration or management, the responsibility in this area also increases. This is true in almost all departments and if suitable timely steps are not taken, court cases may create undue strain and stress. Increasing number of court cases is also becoming a bone of contention between the three main pillars of democracy, namely the legislature, the executive and the judiciary. The tendency of blaming each other for the sorry state of affairs is also increasing. While this may be an agenda for serious discussion in any other forum, no purpose is served by raising it casually in our day-to-day administrative life; that can only worsen the situation and add to our worry with no solution in sight. Therefore, we have no option but to accept the facts and deal with the situation in the best possible manner.

There is also the problem of increasing number of contempt cases. In many of them, personal appearance is also required and that may be very inconvenient, if not embarrassing. This is altogether a different problem, having its genesis in the earlier court cases only. Here are some tips for dealing with these problems in a better manner.

- First, it should be accepted that increased litigation is the result of fast socio-economic changes. While the expectations of the people have increased manifold, the system has not developed sufficiently to cater to them. The prevalence of old procedures, exploitation of the ignorant, increasing loss of values and sheer limitation of the system have added to the gravity of the situation. It is a major agenda which requires substantial structural changes. Such changes will come only with time.

- It is also a fact that people, at large, still have better faith in the judiciary despite all its aberrations particularly at the lower level. In the absence of judicial checks, the other organs of democracy might have played greater havoc with the system. Its co-existence is a must. It is a different matter, however, as to how all the three together could fulfil the aspirations of the people better.
- The judicial process is so cumbersome that, in general, one thinks several times before taking recourse to it. In most of the cases, it is a matter of genuine grievance. If suitable administrative remedy is not given in time, the court cases are bound to increase. It is, therefore, necessary to create an efficient grievance redressal machinery. In most of the cases, it is missing. This fact is also exploited by the vested interests. Many times, a legal case is instituted because there has been lack of communication or because a speaking order has not been passed.
- Once a legal case is filed, it should be paid proper attention at the appropriate level. Clear responsibility should be fixed for this purpose and procedure should be defined. The experience is that most of the legal cases remain unattended at the initial stage and soon they become urgent and complicated. This should not be allowed to happen.
- In bigger departments, a proper monitoring cell should be created to deal with the legal cases and a proper reporting system should be developed in order to draw the attention of appropriate level officers. In no case should the matter be left to lower level officials only.
- A suitable panel of lawyers should be constituted for contesting the cases. Quite often, the cases are decided ex-party, which shows poor management on the part of the department. Proper instructions should be given to panel members to receive notices, etc., on behalf of the department.

Management of Legal Cases

- The panel of lawyers should be as objective as possible and should be reviewed periodically. If done objectively, inefficient or incompetent members can always be dropped. The fee structure should also be realistic and should be reviewed periodically.
- After adverse judgement is passed, there should be proper system to examine whether it is to be complied with or an appeal is to be preferred. Often there is undue delay in taking this decision. In most of the cases, either an appeal is filed indiscriminately or the matter remains unattended. Both create problems later. In the first case, there is loss of time and human resources on the part of the department and harassment on the part of petitioner. In the latter case, it gives rise to contempt cases.
- The general experience is that the petitioner gives sufficient time for the compliance of the order. At times, he is also prepared to give up certain relief, if the order is complied with expeditiously. Only when there is undue delay, he resorts to contempt proceeding. Only in exceptional cases is it done to cause embarrassment to the department or the individual.
- When you receive a contempt notice, it should never be taken as a personal affront. It is against the chair which you hold at a point of time. If you are not on that chair, you have nothing to do with it. It should, therefore, be dealt with objectively. Normally, sufficient time is provided to comply with the order and it should be possible to take suitable decision in that time. In most cases, Courts pass orders for personal appearance only when other methods fail. If the situation is analysed objectively, default is normally found on the part of the department.
- When a notice for personal appearance is received, it should never be resisted mentally. That would help no one. Effort should be made to appear on the first date itself, lest further complications arise. At times, it may not be possible because of other pressing engagements. In that case, your case should be properly represented through an advocate. If done in good

faith, most of the courts agree to your request and fix another date.

- Before appearing in the court, you should study the file yourself and should not depend upon the report of the office, which has a tendency to defend the departmental position. At times, the situation may be altogether different and you may find that justice has not been done to the petitioner. In that case, the departmental stand in the court may have to be modified.

- While appearing in the court, you should be open, confident, well-dressed and sincere. Judges know that you are a senior and responsible officer, though they may appear to be acting otherwise. If the facts are placed before the court with an open mind and helping attitude, the same is appreciated and in most cases the problem is sorted out. Judges can make out your sincerity easily and cooperate in general.

- At times, there may be an ugly situation and you may be reprimanded or even punished. Even the latter is not ruled out these days. These should be taken as the hazards of administrative life. The same should be accepted with dignity and redressal should be sought at the appropriate level. In case you suffer for no fault, it can only be called bad luck. Still the fact is that such a situation arises only in the rarest case.

- Last, being a member of the society, one should be prepared to suffer for its aberrations. If justice is denied in normal course, vested interests will exploit openly, values will, by and large, be given up, and none will come from outside to suffer for them. The victims too will be part of the system, and that is the price one has to pay for belonging to an unjust society. Such errors of the courts should be taken as a divine modality of punishing the members of such an unjust society.

Relations with Colleagues/Peer Group

In my view, the most delicate area is that of relationship with one's own colleagues both within the service and outside. As one enters service, a comparison starts in mind because most of the services have common examination for recruitment. The administrative officers, in particular, carry a feeling of superiority which, if not overcome in time, creates problems. As one goes in the field and occupies important positions like District Magistrate or Commissioner, one comes across officers from technical departments, judicial services, central services and even defence services. To be successful, it is necessary to have cordial relations with all of them. As District Magistrate, the relationship with the Superintendent of Police is also very important and generally affects the quality of administration. Then, there are colleagues in one's own service—senior, contemporary as well as juniors. One has to interact with them in various capacities. All this makes the subject of relationship with colleagues and the peer group very important. If they are not taken care of wisely, one's whole performance and reputation may be ruined as a result of backbiting, jealousies and even mischief. In this regard, the following tips may be useful.

- The first step is to shed away your complex (either superiority or inferiority) at the earliest possible opportunity. One should realise the fact that the entry to a particular service is not only on account of merit but also on account of luck. Today competitions have become so keen that candidates of the same intellectual level may be placed widely in the ultimate selection. As such, if you are selected to a better service, you should not carry the impression that you are necessarily superior in intellect over your friends in apparently less important services. On the other hand, you should consider it to be a greater opportunity to serve the people and a greater responsibility.

- The social or educational background of the members of your family should never be allowed to appear in your relationships with colleagues and the peer group. Once you belong to a common service, you are on an equal footing. This should not only be accepted but also reflected in your dealings.

- It should be remembered that you cannot be friendly with all but it is certainly possible to maintain cordial relations with all. In any case, the effort should be not to have enmity with anyone. At times, an enemy may cause you greater harm than the good caused by many friends. This is possible only when you look at others with a sense of respect and dignity.

- As you become senior in the service, your juniors form opinions about you and the impressions gain currency. It is, therefore, essential to deal with them carefully. They should be treated with dignity, compassion and concern as well as with an attitude of developing them into fine officers. Your personal example is a model for them and for this reason alone, it is necessary to be very careful. A small incident, which you may not even remember, may stick in the memory of your juniors for a long time and they may continue to judge you on that basis.

- Colleagues, who are not much junior to you, may acquire the same position after few years as you do. If their memories about you are not good, it may be reflected in their dealing with you. On the other hand, good memories will have a positive impact on official as well as personal relationship.

- Social visits play an important role in your relations with colleagues and the peer group. If you cultivate this habit in the initial years of service, it goes a long way in building up permanent relations. While closeness may not be there with all, acquaintances are certainly possible. Some of the relations so developed may continue throughout life and may prove more meaningful than your own family relations. With such close friends, you can share your joys and sorrow in true sense.

- While adverse remarks should always be given after due consideration, and rarely, it is more true in the case of junior colleagues of the service. Initial years of their service are meant for guiding and developing them and not for judging them adversely. In a way, it is a test of your own personality and if you fail to develop them into useful officers, you too have to share the blame.

- As far as relations with senior colleagues are concerned, the principles are the same. What you expect from your junior colleagues, your senior colleagues expect from you. While you should be respectful and sincere towards them, a reasonable distance should always be maintained. You should take best care not to annoy them by any of your actions. They may at times not even express their dissatisfaction but may still nurse the grievance. That is the worst situation and should be avoided to the extent possible. Similar attitude should be adopted with their families. Your wife's role in this regard is equally critical.

- Things become little different, when you deal with more senior or junior colleagues. An approximate limit may be plus or minus five years. With this gap in seniority, you have less inhibitions with both, as chances of competition with them are much less. As the gap increases, chances reduce further. Even addressing becomes easier and you can talk with each other more objectively.

- Perhaps the most difficult relationship is with your colleagues close to you in seniority, either senior or junior. With them you have to be more careful, as the chances are that they would concentrate more on your weaknesses rather than strengths. That suits them, in case they have to compete with you at some stage of the career. Therefore, you will have to project yourself as a humble good friend willing to help your colleagues in times of need. It is possible to create an image in due course, which will not create any enmity or jealousy in your colleagues. Yet, if some of them entertain it silently, nothing can be done about it except introspection. If you find nothing wrong with you, it should be taken only as a natural consequence of your being a successful officer.

- Social occasions like birthdays, marriage anniversaries, children's marriages or even calamities, provide good occasions to come closer to each other. They should be attended in all sincerity whenever possible. Your involvement in the joys or sorrows of your colleagues should be genuine. Similarly clubs, service association functions, etc., should also be attended to the extent possible.

- A word about the relation with promoted officers is also important. They are generally elder to you, and may either be little senior or junior in service. In terms of experience, they are superior. It is, therefore, essential that you give due regard to their age and experience and seek their views sincerely. They generally do not compete with you and, therefore, may prove to be better friends.

- The subject of relationship with the officers of other services is in itself a wide one, but few points can be mentioned about them. The most important is the relationship with police and judicial officers when you hold field positions. If you are a member of the IAS, your position is known to everybody and it is foolish to carry a tag of it. Your service only adds to your responsibility and if any relationship goes wrong, you are more responsible than anybody else. If you keep this cardinal principle in mind, things, by and large, will never go wrong. Moreover, you need them more than they need you. After all, if anything goes wrong in the administration, you are the first to be held responsible. The postmortem always comes later.

It is prudent to develop friendly relations with members of the other services like engineering, medical and central services. The initiative in this regard will have to come from you. Once you take the initiative, the response is tremendous. In most of the cases,

Relations with Colleagues/Peer Group

they are the ones who wanted to join your service and had missed it. Therefore, friendship with you is something they look forward to. However, it should be based on sincerity and genuine respect, otherwise it may not last long.

The subject of relations with colleagues and the peer group is a vast one. It is not possible to go into all the intricacies of them within the scope of this chapter. However, with genuine human qualities, you can always deal with them in a healthy manner. In this process, you not only enrich your professional and personal life, but also contribute much better to the system you are meant to serve.

Disposal of Files

The administrative system in India is, in general, notorious for its delays and red-tapism. In fact, the word 'bureaucracy' has almost become a synonym of 'red-tapism'. While the members of the public may not fully understand the compulsions of the system, it is also true that many of these members have a tendency of not taking decisions and keeping matters pending on files. This approach is extremely detrimental to administration and helps no one including those who do so. By doing so, while the dissatisfaction among the public grows, so does the number of files coming to the bureaucracy. It is, therefore, essential that there should be quick and effective disposal of files.

It is worthwhile to mention here that despite many negative aspects of the file system, its merits still outweigh the demerits. My view is that the British rule had shown a great foresight in devising this system, which not only takes care of the accountability aspect, but is also conducive to decision-making based on collective wisdom. It is a different matter that today the needs have changed greatly though the system has not changed accordingly. Further, the fall in the value system has played havoc and in many cases, files either become a tool of exploitation or inaction. But the system in itself is still useful and workable, provided the members are willing to work. In this chapter, an effort is being made to suggest certain tips for effective and quick disposal of files. They are as follows:

- You should understand that a file is not merely a bunch of papers; behind each file, there is a person or a group of persons or the society at large. Their interests are linked with the file. Therefore any file coming to you should be treated with responsibility and with the people's welfare in mind. It may not be important for you, but it is very much so for those who are affected by your comments on the file.

- It should also be understood that your comment should be a step in the direction of decision-taking or problem-solving and not just a means of getting rid of the file. In no case, the disposal of file should be considered as an act of drudgery.
- As far as possible, files should be maintained properly with neat and strong file covers. Unnecessary papers should not be kept on them. The idea is to make a file good-looking so that you feel like dealing with it.
- The movement of a file begins mostly with a receipt in the *dak* or a petition in person. Therefore, it is essential that clear orders are passed on them so that there is no confusion at the lower level. The clearer the orders on the receipt are, the quicker and easier is the processing of the concerned file. This is an important step in the direction of effective disposal.
- The levels, through which a file passes, should not be many. These days there is a great emphasis on this. Generally, only three or four steps are adequate from initiating level to decision-taking level. If stretched beyond this, there is likelihood of delay as well as confusion. One subjective intervention can sabotage or delay the file unnecessarily.
- When the files come to you, their segregation into three categories—routine, important and urgent—is helpful. While the urgent files should be disposed of urgently and routine files leisurely, the important files need greater attention and application. Mostly the delay is in the disposal of such files. This is for two reasons. If you are a busy officer, you may not have enough time to go through them and even if you find time, you may not be willing to take decision in order to shun responsibility. There can be nothing more unfortunate than this. You are there for taking decisions and if you avoid them for any reason, you are no better than your subordinates

or may be even worse. The sooner you get rid of this tendency, the better it is.

- Once you believe in the philosophy of taking decisions, they should be quick. Never delay a decision for fear of committing a mistake. The chances of mistake in a quick decision are no more than in a delayed one. It is also a fact that only those who do not take decisions, do not commit mistakes. But you are not paid for that. You are paid for taking decisions. Despite all the aberrations, the system still protects bona fide mistakes. By inaction, you will only add to the aberrations of the system.

- Some officers have a tendency to write 'Please Speak' or 'Speak' on most of the important files. At times, it may be necessary but if it is done to avoid responsibility or effort, it is bad. Such officers also do not bother to write themselves on the file after the subordinate officer or person has spoken to them. It is left to the subordinate to initiate once again on the basis of conversation with the officer. This may be dangerous and the subordinate may play mischief or commit gross error in reporting the conversation. It is, therefore, necessary that you yourself record your views on the file after conversation.

- Many files have to be referred to departments like law, finance, personnel or someone else. This should be done only when it is essential to do so and not to avoid responsibility. At times, it may be necessary to do so as a matter of strategy. After all, not taking a decision is also a decision sometimes. In case there is a bona fide reference, the file should be followed up by a personal chase at your level or at lower level depending upon the importance of the matter. This helps greatly.

- The language used on the files should always be decent and motivating. In no case anger should be reflected on the file. At best you may show your anguish if someone has acted irresponsibly or foolishly, but never allow your observations to become a talk of the office. This takes away the main

Disposal of Files

issue and instead of any benefit, everyone becomes a loser. Use of words like 'Please' and 'Thanks' should be made lavishly and genuinely. This does wonders and you lose nothing. Occasionally, appreciation should also be expressed. It may bring a lot of change in the attitude at the lower ranks.

- One important factor in the quick disposal of file is communication within the office. If the communication is good, there is coherency in the notings even if the views differ. For this frequent interaction in the form of staff meetings, weekly meetings or informal discussions is very helpful. Differences can always be sorted out in these forums instead of on the file. If you do so, disposal of files becomes much smooth and fast.
- Differing views in the files should be taken very objectively. After all, wisdom is nobody's monopoly and the same problem may have more than one solution. The solution suggested by others may be better than yours. If so, you should readily agree to a different viewpoint unless you have strong reason to stick to yours. In that case, reasons should be recorded nicely and convincingly. This not only keeps harmony but is also in your interest in the long run.
- After a decision is taken on the file, the same has to be converted in the form of an order. Often, there is delay and exploitation in the issue of the orders. Unless this malady is also taken care of, the whole exercise of taking a quick and effective decision on the file may turn out to be futile. Therefore, a suitable system of monitoring in this regard is a must.
- Even when a decision on file is in the negative, it should be conveyed to the applicant. Such a letter should also be convincing and as far as possible, should give reasons for the negative decision. This should also be done promptly so that the applicant may explore other avenues of remedy.
- One point generally raised about the disposal of files is whether they should be carried home or not. My advice is that if your home is not a camp office, then files should not

be brought home unless there are compelling reasons. It is far more expedient to sit in the office a bit late and dispose of the files every day. If for some reason files accumulate, it is better to open office on a holiday and dispose them off. In any case, the effort should be to clear all the files by weekend. Any delay on your part gets perpetuated at lower levels.

- Some officers waste a lot of time in the correction of drafts of the letters or minutes and even in the fair copies. This may cause unnecessary delays and waste of resources. Unless there is gross error of facts or the language, they should be signed. Most of the time, it is more important to convey the message in time rather than seek perfection in the language of the message. The saying that 'The best is the enemy of the good' applies very aptly in such situations.

- While dealing with the file, use should be made of all modern tools available to you. If some points can be clarified over telephone, fax or e-mail, the same should be done promptly at your level only without passing down the file. This helps not only in taking quick and better decision but also improves the office image greatly.

- Last, it is worthwhile to remember once again that disposal of file is only a means and not an end. The end is to give relief to the person or persons behind the file. Therefore, the approach should be positive, solution oriented and humane. Even if the decision is in the negative, it should be with compassion. If you have a reputation of being a fair officer, even your mistakes are accepted without complaint.

Relations with Politicians

One very important area for an administrator is dealing with politicians. Unfortunately, right from the entry in the service, most members of the bureaucracy carry a feeling that this area is the most difficult. They also believe that a politician only interferes and somehow they have to tolerate him. I distinctly remember that as probationers, when we called on the then President of India (Late Shri Faqruddin Ali Ahmed), one lady probationer raised this point. Of course, that was not an occasion for the President to respond but this certainly supports what I am trying to say.

This is very unfortunate and the sooner one gets rid of this feeling, the better it is in everyone's interest. In a democratic set-up, 'politics' and 'administration' are so interwoven that a healthy cooperation between the two is a must for larger welfare. Instead of cooperation, what is happening is either collusion or collision. Both are bad and harm the democratic system. Cooperation can come only when we understand each other and realise that the roles of the two are complementary to each other. The experience is that when treated with respect and understanding, a politician is more cooperative than our own colleagues. Suppose for the sake of argument it is not so, the path of collision or collusion is even worse. In both situations, the chances are greater that we would be the ultimate victim. After all, in a democratic setup, a politician represents the people who are the ultimate masters.

In this background, the subject of relationship between an administrator and a politician becomes very important. If one can deal with them in a proper manner, life becomes easy and administration becomes smooth and welfare-oriented. It does not at all mean that one should always succumb to the demands of the politicians. Far from it. Actually, proper dealing with them is a must for not doing so. When one is genuinely courteous and willing to help, the chances of unreasonable demands are reduced on their own and even if it is so, one can take a firm stand without creating any disharmony. Thus proper management of the politicians is a double-edged weapon for the bureaucrats which not only ensures their survival but also the welfare of the people.

Following are a few tips which are helpful when you deal with politicians:

- The first step is to recognise their importance as representatives of the people, who are supreme in a democratic set-up. Surely they have some qualities in them, otherwise people would not have chosen or elected them as their representatives.
- It is a fact that a politician understands the needs and ethos of the people much better than you do. Howsoever you might try, people are always more open to their representatives than to you. From this viewpoint, their opinion becomes very important for decision-taking.
- Politicians need you as much as you need them. It is difficult for them to say 'no' to those whom they represent. At times they want you to say 'no' on their behalf so that their embarrassment is avoided. But they want this to be done in a manner which protects their position also. There is always an art of saying 'no', which offends none.
- If you are fair to all, politicians respect you. By and large your fairness suits them too, unless you are very rigid. What a politician likes least is your double standard. He opposes it tooth and nail and you will become a victim of your own trait sooner or later. On the other hand, if he believes in your fairness, he will be prepared to wait till he convinces you about his viewpoint.
- The greatest need in the management of a politician is courtesy. This hardly costs anything to you but matters a lot for him. He should not be made to wait unnecessarily, if he comes to see you. Occasionally offering a cup of tea or coffee

is also very helpful, in case you have spare time. Such meetings can be used for gathering important information or for knowing his viewpoint on various matters occupying your mind. Quite often, you arrive at a better decision through such informal consultation.

- Similarly in the matter of telephone calls, you should be easily accessible and courteous. If it is possible to dispose of the matter over telephone, it saves a lot of your and his time. In case you are not in a position to talk to him or his call is received in your absence, the same should be returned within a reasonable time. This will convey your sincerity and then you can be more objective in dealing with his demands.
- When a politician happens to be an elected representative also, he needs even greater attention for reasons more than one. He may be a busy person and in certain matters may require your immediate attention. There may be political compulsions on him which you may not always be able to understand. In that case, some margin to his demands may have to be given in the larger interest. Last, he is in a position to harm you, if you annoy him for some reason whatsoever.
- When a politician also happens to be your direct boss either as minister or non-official chairman, the situation becomes even more delicate. The only advice which may be helpful is, that if you are not in tune with him, it is better to leave that position and take some other assignment. Fighting or finding fault with him all the time helps no one and only serves as entertainment material for your office and others.
- It is a myth that proper dealing with politicians means making compromises. It is the other way round. When you treat them properly, you are in a better position to explain them your viewpoint and thus reduce the chances of making compromises. On the other hand, if you treat them with contempt, you may end up making more compromises. It should, however, be remembered that in a system which is far from perfect, it is futile to expect perfection from

politicians, whose very survival depends upon the existing system. Therefore, occasional adjustments, which do not at all prick your conscience, only add to your grace and dignity. It is rightly said that an administrator should be like mild steel and not cast-iron. Mild steel bends but does not break while the cast-iron breaks but does not bend.

- Some clarifications are required about the word interference itself. When a politician puts up any demand before you, there is a tendency to dub it as interference. This is grossly wrong. A politician is very much a part of the system which you, as a creature of the same system, are meant to subserve. You do not have to behave as if you have monopoly over it. Therefore, any demand from the politician should prima facie be looked upon as the need of the system. My experience is that the demands of our own colleagues, friends and relatives are more difficult to handle than those of the politicians. While at times, one can be firm in dealing with the politicians' demands, it becomes difficult to do so in the case of those who are more near to us. Not only that, saying 'no' to them may make them your enemy for all times to come. Seen from this viewpoint, politicians are a better lot to deal with.

- At times, situations arise when reason does not help and you may have to act tough. There should be no hesitation in doing so. Many politicians may not understand your sincerity or helping attitude and may even exploit the same. Such persons may, occasionally, be given your piece of mind but it should be done without losing temper. Even when you show toughness, the language should be measured and it should only reflect your conviction about your working. By and large, such situations arise rarely.

- Last, as you mature in the service, you build your own reputation and thereafter that reputation helps you a lot. Once you are known as an upright and sincere officer, you will be able to deal with most of the situations in a cordial manner. But if you yourself lack the qualities of a good administrator, no technique will work and sooner or later you will suffer. In that case, how can you blame the politicians ? The blame has to be borne by you. I can say with some conviction that I have hardly faced any problem in dealing with the politicians. I do not know whether they had any problem or not.

Making an Effective Speech

As an administrator or manager one often comes across occasions when he or she has to make a speech. These are the opportunities which can be used to great advantage both for personal development as well as for the larger public interest. The art of making an effective speech comes with experience but the process can always be expedited if some tips are kept in mind. The variety of occasions is so wide that one has to tune oneself accordingly. If this is correct, the chances of the speech being effective increase.

The following tips may be useful in this regard:

- The first step is to accept the fact that making 'Speech' is an essential part of your job. Therefore, any hesitation or shyness should be given up at the earliest possible. Even if you are not a speaker, you have to take the plunge. The earlier you do it, the better it is. It should be kept in mind that knowledge without expression or communication loses its value to a great extent. It is more true in public life where communication plays a very important role and speech is a good means for the same.

- It is always good to do some homework before making a speech particularly when the occasion is known to you in advance. Apart from the relevant facts, the background of the occasion, the expectations of the audience as well as your limitations should be kept in view. At times, it may be helpful to put down your thoughts in writing. This is of great help when you have to speak in the presence of your superiors or important people.

- The length of the speech is very crucial for its effectiveness. If it is a formal occasion, it becomes even more important. If the time is already assigned to you, the effort should be to complete it within the assigned time, unless special conditions arise. In that case, you have to judge the mood and the need of the audience as well as the convenience of the organisers. In no case the impression should be given that you are extending your speech for want of planning or to show your importance.
- The initiation as well as the closing of speech, both are very important. While initiating, it is necessary to address properly taking into account all those who are present. While those sitting on the dais should be addressed respectfully, equal respect should be shown towards those who are not on the dais. If you can spot some dignitary sitting in the audience, an address should be made towards him or her also. However, it should also be kept in mind that the list should not be very long, otherwise it may become boring and repetitive. A careful overall assessment should be made so that protocol, decency and mood, all are taken care of.
- Similarly, while closing the speech, the effort should be to summarise your thoughts without being unnecessarily repetitive. If you have already made a long speech, it is all the more necessary. The idea is that conclusion should be short and crisp. Also a few words of appreciation and gratitude towards those who invited you or those who listened to you should be spoken genuinely. Again, this should also be a short exercise.
- The content of your speech is very important. It should suit the occasion, audience and the time available. There is no point in making a learned speech in the presence of a simple village folk. They want to listen from you about matters of their concern in a manner with which they associate themselves. Similarly, in the presence of a learned gathering, no purpose is served by speaking of routine things or by imposing yourself. By and large, people know your status

and merit and there is hardly any need to prove it by your speech. It is a different matter that your speech may add to them.

- The language of the speech is also important. Whatever be the language chosen, it should be able to pass on your ideas to the audience. Some speakers have the tendency of speaking in very chaste language. It may not always be very effective and the audience may pay more attention to the language than the content. After all, the language is only a means, not an end. However, the mixing of two or more languages should be avoided and should be done only when it is essential to do so.

- Judgement of public mood is a must for effective speaking. The speech should be tuned accordingly. Selective input of humour adds to the interest and concentration of the audience. However, cheap remarks should never be made though it may make the audience laugh. Later this is invariably commented upon adversely.

- Equally important is your body language when you speak. You should pay your attention to the entire audience at a reasonable frequency when you speak. Even if you are reading a written speech, the eyes should be lifted from the paper and turned towards the audience at reasonable intervals. Movement of your hands, legs and the confidence on your face, all are important for making an effective speech. If you are able to display your confidence, your message is received in a more effective and convincing manner.

- Difference of opinion should be expressed in a pleasing manner. You should remember that no single opinion can be absolute and others may be equally right. Therefore, the opinions of others should be treated with respect, while you make your point which should be done with proper reasoning. Even if your point is not established, your respect always increases in this manner.

- Criticism, if at all necessary, should be done carefully. It should never be done in a sarcastic manner. Direct references should be avoided to the extent possible. Speeches are meant for making more friends and not enemies. It should be remembered that truth should be spoken pleasantly and unpleasant truth should not be spoken. It is more true when you speak in public.
- Speech is also an occasion to express your policies, priorities and strategies. Such occasions should, therefore, be fully utilised. Quite often they prove more effective also. You can also convey your firmness, fairness and other administrative qualities through your speech. But it will be effective only when you actually practise what you say in public, otherwise the gain will only be temporary and will lead to greater loss of credibility in the long run.
- If the speech is an in-house exercise, it is equally important. These are the occasions when you can share your views, concerns and doubts with your employees in general. Most of them don't come in your close contact and may have apprehensions which are far from true. Such apprehensions can also be removed during such interactions. My experience is that if you enjoy the confidence of a common employee, it adds to your strength tremendously.
- National festivals like the Independence Day, Republic Day, Gandhi Jayanti, etc., are also the occasions when you are supposed to speak at various forums. They call for sincere words and not the routine ones. Audience can make it out from your body language as well as the oral language. They are also the occasions when emotions of the audience can be utilised for the greater good.
- Last, it should be remembered that a good heart is as important as a good head, when you make a speech. When the words come from your heart, they are much more effective, even if the language is not up to the mark or the voice is not very pleasing. They are subservient to the

sincerity of the words. History is full of examples where great heroes won the people through their sincere words only. Of course, if the sincere words can be coupled with the art of speaking, your words will work not only as magic but also as music.

Relations with the Media

Today the media is the fourth pillar of democracy and all of us have to interact with it whether we like it or not. It also plays an important role in educating the masses, disseminating information and keeping a watch on the other three pillars. However, like any other organ of democracy, it is also not without faults and at times it annoys us. Many of us, therefore, develop a feeling of dislike towards media. Doing so helps nobody. Media is a strong institution and it is neither our job to remove its faults nor is it possible. Let the relevant institutions do that. To the bureaucrats, it should suffice if a meaningful relation is maintained with it. If they do so, media becomes an important tool to be used in the larger interest. Not all bureaucrats are able to do so and even if they are not at fault, they as well as the system suffers. It is certainly possible to avoid such a situation provided certain do's and don'ts are kept in mind. An effort is being made to list them here.

- The first point is to acknowledge the importance of the role of media despite its aberrations. To do so you should try to imagine the scene without media. Perhaps, there will be much more arbitrariness and disorder if media was not there to watch the system. It should also be kept in mind that aberrations are not only in the media but in other organs too. These are institutional problems beyond the capacity of an individual. Their solution may lie elsewhere, but certainly not with the administrative officers.
- You should keep an optimum distance from the media. It should neither be very close nor be very distant. Both are likely to be misinterpreted with you being the ultimate victim. The middle path is the best. You should allow the media to

The middle path is the best. You should allow the media to come to you, if needed, and go to the media, if required. It should be remembered that if information is not fed to it through official means, it will gather the same through unofficial channels. That may be distorted or tempered by vested interests. Every important department should have a responsible person or a cell to deal with the media.

- It is helpful to develop acquaintance with important members of the press and it should be a natural process. Most of them are responsible persons and respond to your need in an objective manner. Exception can always be taken care of or ignored.

- A regular press note, either weekly or monthly, may be issued to the media. It depends upon the nature of activities in your department. It should also be ensured that such a press note is issued only at an appropriate level.

- Today media has an investigative role too. Its investigation may be related to your department. If so, reasonable cooperation should be extended, if you feel that the investigation is in good faith. However, some sort of discretion is called for in such a situation. In any case, the matter should be considered with an open mind.

- The members of the media have the habit of dropping in at any time. While this should be discouraged, one should not be very rigid about it. There are compulsions for them too and their time has its own demands. If this is kept in mind, the situation can always be handled decently. Once you have a sense of respect towards them, they will also understand your compulsion.

- The members of the press should be given equal treatment. Any inclination in favour of somebody or otherwise may be counter-productive. If non-cooperation comes from a certain media, it can be taken care of in a natural way and, at times, by making no secret of it.

- One should never use the media for personal image-building. It is very dangerous. You will soon create many enemies both within and outside who may cause greater damage than what you may gain by sponsored publicity. Similarly, one has to remain impersonal towards the criticism also. It should not be forgotten that most of the time the media addresses the institution or the chair and not the person. It calls for an introspection and if after introspection you find your conduct to be without fault, the matter should be overlooked. In all probability, time will take care of it.

- Personal interviews should be carefully agreed to and with all sense of responsibility. The objective should be to highlight the achievements of the organisation without being personal about them. There is no greater pleasure than to give the credit of good performance to others and to take the responsibility of lapses onto oneself. In any case, everyone can read between the lines and in the process, you only earn goodwill as well as respect.
- Occasional talks on radio or TV should also be accepted in the normal course. At times, they may require extra effort on your part but it is worth doing. Apart from the dissemination of information to public, it adds to your confidence, makes you known and fetches some money too. It may be used for surprise gifts to family members or friends.
- If your department has funds for publicity, then your role becomes even more difficult. It helps to frame a clear advertisement policy and to follow it in a fair manner. There may be occasional variations which can be levelled out in the long run. Engagement of a good publicity firm is helpful in situations of commercial needs.
- One difficult task is to deal with the small newspaper organisations. There are too many of them and some may be unduly fussy. You have to be firm with them, though considerate at the same time. They have their own importance and cater to a certain sector of the society which may not be relevant to your organisation. Moreover, they survive on advertisements only and so they may be entertained occasionally. It helps to earmark a certain portion of the

publicity budget for such newspapers which may be used in an objective manner to the extent possible.
- At times, it may be necessary to make use of Press Council Act. This Act provides certain restrictions on the media. While in actual practice such a step is rarely required, it definitely helps in maintaining meaningful relationship with the press.

Last, you should not be unduly worried about adverse publicity. The society we live in is complex and many good as well as bad forces work in it. While mostly it is in our hands not to do anything which may bring bad name to us, it may not always happen like that. At times, one gets defamed for no fault and also gets fame for no reason. Both should be accepted as facts of life. Ultimately, it is your character which defends you in the long run. Anyhow, with time all good and bad things are forgotten and you remain what you are.

Managing Personal Affairs

It has been my experience that while most of us manage our official affairs very well, we fail to do so when it comes to personal affairs. The main reason is that right from the beginning we are made to feel so important that attention towards personal affairs is considered to be very trivial. Most of us are dependent on office even for preparing salary bills, TA bills, etc., that we do not even learn to maintain proper record of our personal matters. No wonder, most of us make a mess of our provident fund account, income tax account, property returns, etc. At times this puts us in great difficulty and we have to spend much more time and energy in sorting out these matters. It is, therefore, essential to pay attention towards these matters right from the beginning so that no difficulty may arise in future. In this chapter some tips will be given for managing your personal affairs.

- Service Record: It is advisable to open a service record file as soon as you enter the service. This file may start with the cutting of the newspaper in which your result is published and all subsequent documents received in connection with the service may be kept on this. These documents may include posting orders, charge certificates and other personal correspondence with the Government. After every 5 to 10 years an exercise can be taken to weed out some papers from the file so that it remains manageable. Such file is very useful for preparing bio-data and also the service record which is asked for by Appointment Department/Personnel Department, from time to time. This file may also contain your pay slips received from AG Office.

- Provident Fund Record: You become a member of Provident Fund soon after joining service. For this you have to file an application on prescribed proforma and nomination forms are also to be filed. Copies of all these can be kept on this file. Thereafter, account slip is received from AG Office every year. In all probability there are some missing credits and correspondence is to be made to get them traced. This should be done promptly otherwise it becomes very difficult to keep Provident Fund Account up-to-date. A certified record of withdrawals from the Treasury should also be obtained wherever you are posted. Extracts of these statements are very useful while updating the Provident Fund Account. Extra copies of letters sent to AG Office should be prepared because it is very unlikely that response would be received on first letter. At times, an official has to be sent to AG Office and once a while you should also try to visit yourself.
- GIS File: There is a General Insurance Scheme of the Government, of which you become member on joining the service. Proper record of subscriptions under this scheme should also be maintained in a separate file.
- Important GOs File: After joining the service you receive many Government Orders relating to personnel matters. Some of them are important and a copy of them should be kept on a file for future use. Once in a while these GOs should be looked into and unnecessary ones should be weeded out.
- Property File: You have to file a return of Movable and Immovable property at the time of joining the service. It is useful to maintain a separate file in this regard as returns has to be filed every year thereafter. The returns should be sent promptly after Government Instructions are received. Record of immovable property can also be kept in this file. Under All-India Service Conduct Rules, any transaction of movable property beyond a certain limit is to be intimated

to the Government. This should be kept in mind and complied with.

- Leave account: You are entitled to 12 Casual Leaves and two Restricted Leaves in a year. Besides this 30 Earned Leaves and 20 Half-pay leaves accrue every year. Then, there is a provision of leave encashment in certain states. It is very useful to maintain record of all these leaves. This can be done on a diary. From time to time a record of leave balance can be asked from AG Office or Controlling Office (wherever it is maintained) and tallied with your own record. A proper leave record helps you to plan your holidays, etc. better.

- Training File: Nowadays there is great emphasis on in-service training. You are sent for one-week as well as three-week training periodically. Government expects that training courses should be attended without default and great importance is attached to it. It is advisable to maintain a separate file for correspondence in connection with training programmes. Quite often, you have to indicate the training courses attended. Such filing is very helpful.

- Income Tax File: Income Tax may not be a very important matter in the beginning of the service but it becomes so, as you become senior. Most of the officers do not apply their mind in computing Income Tax and pay unnecessary tax. The provisions in regard to salaried persons are very simple and once understood, there is no need of depending on your office. You will always be in a better position to plan your investments and save Income Tax. Also returns should be filed within prescribed time. If it is possible to have a permanent address in the state of your service, the return can be filed in the Income Tax Office consisting that address. This will make your returns consistent and many things may not be required to explain year after year.

- LIC File: Most probably, you will get yourself insured after entering the service. At times there may be one or more policy. A proper record of these policies and correspondences in regard to them is necessary. For this a separate file should be opened and maintained.

- **Investment File:** An officer, these days, has to plan his/her investments properly so that the salary income can be augmented. A proper record of your investment is necessary so that you are able to take timely decisions regarding withdrawal and reinvestment, etc. A consolidated record of the investment should also be prepared every year.
- **ACR File:** Annual Confidential Reports are very important in the service. Nowadays, there is a system of self-assessment which every officer is supposed to submit to the Reporting Officer. A copy of self-assessment should always be maintained in a file. Any subsequent correspondence, if necessary, say in the case of adverse remarks, should be made from this file. Also relevant documents which form the basis of self-assessment should be kept on this file. Documents from this file may be weeded out after an interval of five to ten years. Similarly, a file should be maintained of all adverse remarks given by you to your subordinate officers. In all probability, a representation against such remarks may be received and you could be required to give your comments. Maybe, by that time, you are transferred and may not have access to the relevant documents. Maintaining such documents in your own file is very useful at that time.
- **File of important letters:** During your service you receive many important letters from various sources. Some of them are worth preserving. A file may be maintained for such letters. They are very interesting to go through after a lapse of time. The periodic weeding of such letters should also be done as some of them may be only of contemporary importance.
- **Record of TA Bills:** Though it is not very necessary, there is no harm in keeping a brief record of your travelling along with ticket numbers, etc. The TA claims may also be noted down. At times, this information turns out to be very useful.

- Miscellaneous matters: Apart from the important personal affairs, there are many miscellaneous personal matters which should be managed properly in order to be a successful administrator. These are:
  - (a) Greeting letters: You receive greeting letters, cards on various occasions from different sources. Quite often, these messages are due to your official position. You should make sure that all these messages are responded to in time. If you develop a system of prompt response, it will hardly add to your work and at the same time will earn you a lot of goodwill. Similarly, you should not forget to send such messages to others and in time. For this, a timely preparation is necessary. Generally, there are enough resources available to you and it is only a question of giving timely and proper instructions.
  - (b) General letters: Since you are a member of an important service, people consider it prestigious to correspond with you. The letters will come to you from friends, relatives and even public. Quite often, these letters are for seeking a favour or recommendation. You should not mind it. This is what makes you important. However you should apply your discretion and need not oblige everyone. Though a courteous and prompt reply should always be given. The experience is that a letter is generally the fastest mode of communication. There is no need of making a telephone call or sending a telegram, if a postcard or an envelope can serve the purpose. It is worthwhile to write some letters in your own handwriting.
  - (c) Maintenance of bio-data: As a member of the service you are quite often invited to preside over various functions. The organisers generally ask for your bio-data at short notice. You should keep them ready and provide a copy to them. The bio-data should be updated from time to time.

(d) Preparation for speeches: Quite often, you are required to deliver speeches at various forums. While most of them can be extempore and may not require any preparation, some speeches require prior preparation. This should be done seriously. Relevant data / information for speeches should be collected in time and contemplated upon. At times, speech may have to be reduced in writing also. A good speech always brings lot of goodwill. Also the length of the speech should be optimum.

(e) Record of house allotment, electricity bills, etc.: Miscellaneous file for these matters can be kept, as you are in a transferable service. This saves you from many difficulties due to lack of systems in the concerned departments. Papers related to gas connection, etc. can also be kept on this file.

(f) Record of books: All of us have a number of personal books depending upon individuals' liking. Book-reading is a very good habit and should be promoted. It is always useful to have a proper record of your books and they should be kept in such a manner that they are accessible to you. This will help you in planning your reading and also save them from non-serious borrowers.

I have attempted to cover all possible aspects of personal affairs while there may be some more also. My personal experience is that proper management of personal matters is very important and it saves you from a lot of worries. The time and effort spent for managing these affairs is always worthwhile.

Managing Stress

Today the word 'Stress' has become almost synonymous with 'Development'. As we are developing externally in the scientific and material fields, coping internally is becoming equally difficult, leading to growing stress. This has substantially taken away the pleasures of life despite all physical possessions. Those in administrative services are worse sufferers, as they have to face the brunt of the social tensions almost all the time. The subject of 'Stress Management', therefore, assumes great importance and needs to be analysed thoroughly before arriving at a suitable management plan. The subject can be addressed from different viewpoints, namely, medical, psychological, economic, social, etc. No doubt that all these factors combined together, are responsible for stress generation. Central to all these are the attitudes and thoughts of an individual. That is why the same situation creates different responses in different persons. In other words, the perception of the same situation varies from person to person. Some look at the positive side of the situation, while others look at the negative side. Surely, there is a better way of dealing with the same situation and if we can tune ourselves for better response, managing stress becomes easy.

The first step in this direction is to accept stress as a fact of life. There is no need for struggling stress, as it will only make its handling more difficult. Whether we wish or not, the pressures of modern life are bound to create stress and we have to learn its management. It is like a guest who has come to our home without our consent or prior information. No purpose is served by spoiling our mood in such a situation and in all probability, such a response will only worsen it. What is required is an intelligent handling of the situation in order to get rid of the unwanted guest. The same is true of the stress also. In fact, the whole dynamics of life is due to stress. In other words, it is a sign of life, of being awake. No progress in life is possible without some amount of stress. It is a part of our evolution as well as physical development. It also keeps our motivation alive. Thus, there are many positive aspects of stress, which we need to understand and accept. If stress is present in optimum measure and right direction, it only adds to the pleasures of life. Harm is caused only when it is excessive or wrongly directed.

Having understood the positive and negative sides of stress, we may now list out some situations which are the potential causes of stress. There may be a large number of them but some of them can be listed as below:

a) meeting difficult targets or deadlines;
b) unreasonable boss;
c) loss in business;
d) loss of job or unemployment;
e) accident/death;
f) sudden or grave illness;
g) family problems;
h) overwork or pressure of time;
i) difficult place of posting;
j) natural calamity;
k) misbehaviour by some dear or near one;
l) wrong allegation, misunderstanding or communication gap;
m) riots or strike;
n) undue litigation.

All these situations are clear in themselves and need not be explained in detail. The idea is to convey that in life there are always chances of stress. We have to learn not to become its victim. And for that, we need to develop a positive attitude towards life. After all, when we ourselves set difficult targets or take risks in order to make life more enjoyable, why should we complain when Nature creates such situations? We must welcome them because they provide an opportunity to test us and to better our performance. A successful person always sets higher targets in life, whatever be the struggle involved. That only gives him true pleasure. Difficult situations provided by Nature should also be seen in this perspective and if we do so, life becomes harmonious and pleasant. On the other hand, if we fall victim to them, life becomes an agony causing undue stress.

We should always remain alert to the symptoms of excessive stress so that timely remedial steps may be taken. In short they are:

a) loss of concentration;
b) loss of energy;
c) loss of enthusiasm;
d) sleep disturbance;
e) negative thoughts;
f) irritation or anger;
g) headache;
h) lack of interest in life.

As soon as these symptoms show their presence, we should be alert and take steps to deal with them in a rational manner. Though development of positive attitude towards life is a long process, it has to begin through a contemplative process. If the process is continued, very little else is required for stress management. In fact, the other measures are effective only when the attitude is positive. Here are some of the steps to deal with the stress:

- The first step is the acceptance itself. We need not unduly fight with the stress and should take it as a fact of life. Everyone has a good share of it but we only know of our share and carry the delusion that others don't have it. In fact, others may be worse victims than us.
- The next step is to analyse the cause of stress. If done objectively, quite often the problem will cease to exist or the solution will appear with it.
- If the solution is not in sight, write down the possible consequences and mark the worst scenario. Accept it

mentally and be prepared to face it. Thereafter, whatever happens would be better than what we are prepared for.

- When solutions are in sight, write them down and choose the best one. Then act on it. There are good chances that it will work and the problem will be solved. Remember that we can do only our best, but the result is not in our hands.
- Sometimes, what we wish or expect is much less than what is in store for us and the failures may only be a route to that. When we get that we will laugh at our failures and thank God for the same.
- Look for an opportunity in every situation. Difficult situations are created by Nature only for that purpose. Normally, we fail to see the game of Nature and waste our time and energy in blaming it. We forget that no great person in the world has escaped difficult situations and that their greatness has been the result of facing them with courage and wisdom. Remember that extraordinary things happen in the lives of extraordinary people only.
- Our body plays an important role in the management of stress. We should treat it well and cultivate good habits right from the beginning. However, it is never too late. Regular physical exercise like jogging, morning walk, a game of tennis or golf keeps the stress away. Later on, habit of contemplation, concentration and meditation should be cultivated. They are best protection against stress and add to the pleasures of life.
- All of us have friends and close relatives. They are for a purpose and the purpose is to share our joys and sorrows with them in true sense. While our joys multiply by sharing, sorrows are divided by doing so. Both help in reducing stress. If we cannot do so, we have no business to call them friends or relatives and it is better not to have them. As a matter of fact, today's nuclear family system is greatly responsible for increasing stress.
- Keeping meaningfully busy is a good way of avoiding stress, as an empty mind is a devil's abode. However, our schedule

should be healthy. Also avoid hastiness. If at a point of time, there are more demands on our time, they should be asked to stand in queue. In any case, we cannot attend to more than one thing at a time. It helps to spend some time in the morning to organise the day's activities.

- Our living habits should be moderate. That only leads to peace and happiness. Stress is an indication of the fact that there is something wrong with our habits. If we analyse the situation in an objective manner, we will find that generally peace is a victim of trivial matters and we pay too much attention to them. This should be stopped and we should remember that small things are not worth dying for.
- Another golden rule for avoiding stress is to learn living in present. Most of us spoil our present in the memories of the past or worries of the future. While it is good to learn from the past and to plan for the future, dwelling in them is counter-productive. Our concentration should be on the present, which is the living moment.
- Develop a good sense of humour. It is very helpful in avoiding stress. Things always do not happen the way we would like them to. We have no control on others and their actions may hurt us. At times, even our own actions hurt us. It helps to laugh them away, if nothing else is possible. Humour can save us from many disturbing situations, if we know how to apply it.
- These days, most of us believe that being good and truthful is counter-productive. This is a great mistake. We should understand the value of these qualities in the right perspective and should not measure them in terms of currency. Lack of them is a potential cause of stress. Natural living demands being good and truthful. The good thing about truth is that we don't have to remember it. It does not put undue pressure on our memory, thus saving us from stress. It is always beneficial to be good and trustworthy. Also good qualities of others should be appreciated and this appreciation should be expressed with an open heart. It hardly costs anything but pays rich dividends.

- All worldly events are transitory and this should be kept in mind while analysing our difficulties. Everything passes away with time. Good as well as bad events of life are equally forgotten in due course. If so, there is no point in worrying too much on bad events. Looked at differently, bad events are only gateways to good events. Good events give joy only in the backdrop of bad events. Without them, contrast will be lost and we shall cease to see good even in the so-called good events.
- We must understand life in totality. A partial view may not give the correct picture. In totality it is a wonderful opportunity provided we understand it properly.
- Last, we should have a goal or purpose in life. Our problems become dwarfed in the backdrop of our goal. The chances of stress in a purposeful life are much less. We hardly find a person, who has a purpose in life, having negative thinking.

All these steps are nothing but a process of developing positive thinking. A positive thinker considers himself or herself as a part of the whole. When a large number of people adopt this approach, there is greater prosperity and happiness in the society. In such a society the chances of stress get reduced at individual level as social and economic causes of stress are taken care of. In a way, there is no difference between positive thinking and value-based thinking. Thus, value-based life is the foundation of stress-free life.

Health Management

One important aspect of 'Stress Free Management' which is generally not talked about is 'Our Health'. Only when we remain healthy, we can perform our work well. Our health also has a direct bearing on our happiness. When we remain happy, our work not only becomes excellent, it becomes stress-free too. Therefore, it is necessary to pay attention towards our health. Here are some points which help us in remaining healthy.

- First of all we will have to understand the importance of our body. The proof of our existence on this earth is our body only. All our joys or sorrows are experienced through our body only and they loose their meaning without it. Therefore, it is very necessary to keep it healthy. Only in a healthy body dwells a healthy mind, intellect and spirit.

- The chances of positivity are more in a healthy person in comparison to an unhealthy person. It we pay right attention to our health, there are more chances of objectivity in our life and it becomes easier for us to grow in an integrated manner.

- Though our bodies vary in shape, colour and size, essentially we all are the same. These features of our body generally depend upon our genes and we hardly have any control on them. Yet by proper upkeep, we can certainly give a better look to our body.

- Nature has designed our body in such a manner that by living within reasonable parameters we can keep it healthy to a great extent. Nature has also given us the liberty of crossing these parameters occasionally. Only when we cross them frequently, it is affected adversely. This way we are ourselves responsible for our health to a great extent.

- The second important aspect of our health is our food. Nature is very liberal and just in this respect also. As soon as a child is born, food is made available to him/her in the form of mother's milk. At that time this milk is his/her complete food. As we grow, mother Nature provides us with different kinds of necessary food materials. Nature also ensures that right food is available to us at right time. If we understand this law of Nature, we can keep our body healthy by taking seasonal natural food.

- Our body accepts natural food best and remains healthy in the process. If we eat more than the requirement of the body or the kind of food is not in conformity with it, the body resists the same.

- Our falling sick is an indication of the fact that somewhere we are going against the Nature. Thus sickness is a means of cautioning us to change our habits or daily routine. Even then if we don't pay attention to it, bad health is a natural consequence and Nature cannot be blamed for the same.

- We should also remember that our body needs only a small quantity of right food. Food, more than what is required, becomes a burden on the body and expedites the process of its decay. It has been rightly said that half the food we take, keeps us alive and the other half takes us to the doctors.

- Apart from food, our other habits too affect our health. These include exercises, entertainment, sleep, smoking, drinking, daily-routine, etc. If we develop good habits right from the beginning, they have positive effect on our health. Nature gives us enough liberty in this respect also and we can completely stop following them for some time or partially for longer time without causing much harm to our health. But it is a fact that restraint in all these areas is necessary for good health. Our body needs sleep, exercise, etc., in optimum quantity and a healthy routine is helpful in this respect. Those

who understand these needs of the body and care for them, remain healthy.
- Another important part of our health is our environment. Life on planet Earth exists because of the right environment available here. If this environment is polluted, it is bound to have adverse impact on our health and life. The atmosphere around us has a certain chemistry which is most conducive to our life. To the extent our atmosphere remains natural, our health will also be good.
- Nature has not only provided us the right atmosphere but also the right kind of water. If we pollute it through our unnatural acts, we have to pay the price in the form of our health. Nature has given us sufficient freedom in this respect also and has accordingly provided security mechanism in our body. Our health is adversely affected only when the pollution exceeds tolerable limits. Therefore, our effort should be to live in a natural environment, as far as possible. Those who occupy more responsible positions in the society have greater responsibility in this area too.
- The last but very important aspect of good health is the quality of thoughts we entertain and our attitude. Thoughts have a direct bearing on our health, so it is essential that we always feed ourselves with positive thoughts. The process also should be natural. Once we understand the basic principles of life and know its goal, positive thinking becomes a natural process. It is not difficult to understand that negative thinking has an adverse effect on our life. Therefore, a positive attitude is a must for good health.

If we keep the above points in mind, it is not difficult to remain healthy. The fact is that in that case we shall be healthy without any effort. In that situation we shall be in a position to discharge our duty proficiently as well as efficiently. All modern management institutes and organisations today insist on good health of managers as well as workers. They also make special efforts for the same as it is in the interest of the organisation too. If it is not done loss is twofold: one in productivity and two in reimbursing medical bills.

Say Goodbye to Anger

'Anger' and 'Tension' can be said to be twin brothers. They are born almost simultaneously. When we talk of 'Positive Management' it also implies that we have to say good-bye to our anger. This is a difficult area but very much worth the effort. Higher the position we occupy, the greater is the need of keeping our anger in control. Our anger not only has an adverse effect on us but also on those who work around and with us. In this chapter, effort is being made to analyse the subject of anger and suggest some ways to make it our slave instead of we becoming its slave.

So much is said and written about anger. The Oxford Dictionary defines anger as extreme displeasure. It is always considered to be an undesirable trait. While it is very obvious when taken from religious, spiritual, moral or physical point of view, it is not so when seen from worldly viewpoint. One tends to feel that in a world we face today, it is difficult to survive without anger. Perhaps I also used to feel that way and I used to be angry quite often. It is not that this has been completely won over, but the frequency has reduced greatly. It has not been so as a matter of surrender or helplessness but definitely as a result of wisdom and experience. Now I am of firm belief that anger is not needed even from worldly viewpoint. This is what we are going to discuss in this chapter.

First of all, let us analyse the cause of anger. Whenever we face a situation which is not to our liking, anger is the result. Therefore, in order to avoid the cause of anger, we should always face situations to our liking. Obviously, it is not possible. One may have control over oneself but it is not possible on others. Moreover a situation liked by us may not be liked by others and vice versa. That is to say, that we have to often face situations which we may not like and they become the cause of our anger. It may be indiscipline of a subordinate, disobedience by children, a reprimand from the boss, misbehaviour of a shopkeeper, sudden absence of a servant, a traffic jam, long waiting for a bus or train, etc. There can be countless such occasions which may not be to our liking and are potential causes for our anger.

All this means that in our lives, causes of anger are always present. Does it mean that we should be angry whenever such a situation arises? Let us see how that helps. First of all, let us recall that anger means extreme displeasure and not merely displeasure. Here the word 'extreme' is important. I cannot remember even a single incidence in my life where expressing anger helped. The simple reason is that one becomes more vulnerable after expressing anger. This helps neither the person nor the situation. The moment one gets angry, he loses his discriminating power and chances of taking wrong decisions or actions increase. In all probability, the angry person ends up suffering more than he would have normally suffered.

One may now ask whether feeling angry and not expressing it would be a better proposition. It is certainly better than the earlier situation but even in feeling angry one suffers. First, it is not good for health and, second, it also impairs one's discriminating power. The anger always takes away objectivity.

Then how should one behave in such situations? I think the answer lies in the definition of 'anger' itself. It says anger is 'extreme displeasure'. I feel by removing the word 'extreme' we get the answer. It means there is no harm in feeling displeased in a situation which you do not like. There is no harm in expressing your displeasure in a suitable manner. In fact, it should be done. Whether it is your child, subordinate or any member of the society, whenever situation demands, displeasure should be expressed in a suitable way. Here it will be advisable to remember the famous proverb: 'Truth should be spoken pleasantly and unpleasant truth should not be spoken'. In all likelihood a pleasantly spoken truth will help both you and the situation. The secret is that when you are not extremely displeased you do not lose your discrimination.

In that situation, it is possible to take even strict action without any harmful effect.

A more important question is how to avoid anger. This cannot be done suddenly. One has to gain wisdom as well as experience to win over anger. However, reading of good literature, attending discourses of saintly persons and avoiding situations which are likely to cause anger always accelerate the process. Here, I will mention of a talk on the subject 'Burn Anger Before Anger Burns You' by Dada J. P. Vaswani delivered in Delhi in October 1991. Subsequently it has appeared in the form of a book also. I had the opportunity to listen to him and he summarised his talk beautifully by suggesting 10 points for controlling anger. These are given below:

- Realise that every being is part of God. If so, there is no place for anger as one does not lose temper on oneself.
- See the grace of God in all happenings. Who knows that a situation causing anger in you may be a blessing in disguise?
- Develop forgiveness. Understand that most of the time the person appearing to provoke you, has no such intentions. Even if it is so, forgive him. It will defeat his purpose.
- Keep silent. It very often burns anger.
- Think from the viewpoint of the other person. Believe that no single viewpoint is absolute. There may be other viewpoints too. You will then not be angry if your viewpoint is not accepted.
- Do not overload yourself or feel overloaded. This is one great cause of anger. Attend to one matter at a time. The rest can wait. In any case, it is of no use worrying about them while dealing with one.
- Avoid haste. Plan your work properly so that there is no need of haste.
- Avoid the unpleasant situations. Quite often the anger can be avoided by avoiding the situation. There is no harm in leaving the scene causing irritation.

- Recite a Mantra. This a very powerful way of overcoming anger. Your mind gets occupied with better thoughts.
- Count numbers. If you are angry count up to ten and if very angry, count up to hundred.

These are some very useful and practical tips and if one is really concerned about his anger, these may be of great help. In the end, I would like to mention another famous proverb about anger which is like this:

'If you are right, you can afford not to be angry.

If you are wrong, you cannot afford to be angry.'

Thus there is no need of anger in any situation. This is all the more necessary in the area of management.

Develop an Integrated Personality

Our personality has a direct bearing on our work. It matters even more in case of managers who are often in public contact. Many times we have to face situations when we are held responsible for certain lapses without any fault or mistake on our part and we have to pay a price for the same. In such a situation, if our personality is weak, we can spoil our future by getting disappointed or worsen the situation by loosing our balance. It is therefore necessary for a good manager to develop an integrated personality. This chapter is being devoted to this aspect of the management. If we understand the word 'personality' in a wider perspective stress-free management becomes easy.

Each person has a distinct personality. Some features of the personality impress us and some not. We all want to have an attractive personality but very few understand the necessary aspects of it. For most good personality means to look handsome and prosperous from outside and they pay no attention to the development of the inner self. That is why despite having high intellect, several administrators or managers often have a bad reputation. In the process, neither the individuals are benefited nor the society. On the other hand, a person with an integrated personality is not only an asset for the society, but he himself, remains happy and peaceful apart from being successful. He is also an inspiration for others.

When we talk of an integrated personality, it refers to a personality that has more than one component. Only when all the components are adequately developed, does the personality become integrated or total. What are these components and what are the

Develop an Integrated Personality

characteristics attached to them? We shall use the word 'dimension' in place of 'component' in order to give it a large scope. Here is a brief discussion on each.

The first dimension of our personality is 'physical'. It relates to our body, state of health, appearance, etc. Though this dimension is very important, we have little control over it. By and large, the shape, size and the colour of our body is determined by our genes. The only thing in our hands is to maintain it well in order to remain healthy. For this, a certain discipline is required in our habits. If we cultivate good habits, the body becomes an asset and the development of other dimensions of the personality becomes easier. For example, early rising and early to bed, simple food, regular exercises and cleanliness are habits which keep our bodies healthy. A healthy body generally also means a healthy mind. If the body gives trouble, it becomes difficult to concentrate on other things. Therefore, the development of other dimensions of the personality is also dependent on this dimension which may become less important once the other dimensions develop.

The second dimension of our personality is 'mental'. It relates to the mind which is superior to the body. Thus, this dimension of the personality is superior to the first one. It is the mind which works behind our sense organs. The eye cannot see if the mind refuses to accept the signals and so is the case with other sense organs. Similarly, the mind is capable of making our sense organs indulge in right or wrong activities. Thus, proper development of the 'Mental Dimension' is very important for using the powers of the physical body. It is the mind which makes us educated, skilled in our jobs and enthusiastic about our progress. Those who apply their minds in the right direction, achieve success in their goals. Some of us become doctors, engineers, businessmen or administrators according to our mental make-up. It is mainly the mental dimension which gives us the capacity to take care of our physical needs. But to say that personality development stops here is not correct. We have to add something more to our personality in order to make it integrated and this takes us to the third dimension.

Before we come to the third dimension, some elaboration is necessary. We all know that certain doctors are very kind, sympathetic and helpful while others are not so. It may be that someone in the latter category is more competent professionally but in terms of personality, the compassionate doctor is always considered to be better. The same goes for other professions also. We always prefer a person who is good, kind, helpful and courteous even if those who are not so, are mentally or professionally more competent. This establishes the fact that there is a superior dimension of personality over the mental one. This dimension is known as 'intellectual'. As said earlier, the mind, though superior to the sense organs, is capable of playing mischief if not controlled by a superior faculty. This faculty is called the 'intellect'. It is the intellect which gives us the wisdom to discriminate between good and bad. Obviously, a person with such wisdom has a better personality compared to a person which makes us capable of better judgement and, therefore, useful, also for the society at large. In the process, we earn respect and are considered to be good.

To add perfection to our personality, some finer qualities have to be acquired, even by good persons who may also suffer if they do not strive for them. This dimension of the personality is the 'spiritual' one, the highest dimension. It is a fact that the world we live in is transitory. Even our good deeds are forgotten with time. Therefore, there is a need to transcend them too. If we do not do so, the same goodness may become a cause of misery. Also, goodness is only a relative term and its perception varies with persons and time. We do not get the same response from all persons, even for our good behaviour or virtues. Therefore, a sense of detachment has to be developed towards our good qualities too. It has been seen that many good and successful persons suffer just because they lack this aspect of the personality. One has to accept that all our actions are only a means to an end and the end is self-realisation. Those who understand this reality, develop the spiritual dimension at the right time and are fully prepared for all the eventualities of life. This dimension is thus superior to the earlier three dimensions and is necessary for the complete integration of the personality.

The idea, without going into more details, is to convey that for an integrated personality, all dimensions are necessary. They, of course, generally follow the order in which they have been described. I consider these four aspects like the four legs of a table which give it stability. Though a table with three or less number of legs may appear to be stable, any push or pressure will destabilise it. Similarly, a person with any of the dimensions missing may appear to be stable but is vulnerable to any accident in life which may disturb his equilibrium.

It is only a person with all the four dimensions developed, who can maintain cool in all circumstances and thus lead a stress-free life whether professional or personal.

The Goal of Human Life

Whatever has been said in this book so far, may generally appear to be impractical and we may give several arguments against them. It cannot be denied that many obstacles come on the path of virtue and therefore, it is natural to raise a question as to why one should follow such a path. We get the correct answer to this question only when we have a large view of life. If our thinking or attitude is constricted, we shall never fully accept that following the path of virtue is in our own interest. Here we shall discuss this aspect so that our dilemma is removed completely and we follow such a path without any doubt or hesitation. For this it is essential to understand the importance and goal of human life.

There are millions and millions of creatures living on this Earth. If the plant kingdom is also added to it, the number increases further. Man is just one of them, but the most unique one. Why is it so, should be the question that should occur to everyone who aspires for positive living. Most scriptures say that there exists a cycle of life and death, and in this cycle, one takes birth as a human being once in millions of years. Some scriptures say that human birth takes place after passing through 8.4 million species. No one has the means or capacity to verify these pronouncements, but certainly they are pointers to something very important and significant. And this leads us to the importance of human birth, which is taken for granted by most of us. The fact is that it is one of the rarest opportunities available to us and if we do not make full use of it, nothing can be more unfortunate. I feel that making good use of life is what may be called Positive Living. It implies living for a purpose, for growth and for further evolution. A life so lived is bound to be harmonious and peaceful, otherwise it is a torture and a waste of the unique chance available to us as human beings.

How does man differ from other living creatures of the Earth? We all know the process of evolution behind this development, which itself took millions of years, starting from the Ape Age. The most significant feature of a human being is his capacity to think and discriminate. These two qualities put him on a much higher pedestal vis-à-vis other creatures of Nature. As a result, man is regarded as the most outstanding species among all others and the master of Nature's show. The severity of the Earth's terrain, the depths of the oceans and the distances of the sky are no more a constraint on him. He has penetrated through them all. Today, he is able to communicate throughout the Earth with the push of a button, to forecast various phenomena of Nature to a great accuracy, to take care of most of the diseases and has plenty to eat. All this has changed his life beyond recognition. What to say of future generations, today, human life is transforming every moment. It should be a matter of envy for other species, but is it really so? The answer is not so simple, rather, it becomes a matter of contemplation.

What is wrong with the power of thinking and discrimination that a human being is equipped with? The greatest wrong is that with such power at his command, man soon starts differentiating himself from Nature. He forgets that it is this same Nature which has given him such powers and starts using them against his benefactor itself. Nature may tolerate it for some time, but soon the misuse of these powers rebounds on him and he falls a victim to it. When such a thing happens, human life becomes a curse instead of being a boon. Under delusion, man also fails to take timely corrective steps and wastes this wonderful scope of enjoying as well as growing. Thus, he becomes a loser on both fronts and instead of evolving further, he takes a rebirth to repeat the process. It is like killing oneself with the same weapon that is meant to protect and lead one on the path of progress. Such a life is a negative living.

As said earlier, making good use of the life and its gifts available to us is positive living. For this also, the same thinking and discrimination are the basic tools. The difference lies only in their use. While a negative life means living apart from Nature, a positive life is a part of it. A positive thinker sees no conflict with Nature, which is a manifestation of the Supreme Being, rather he finds it conducive for his further growth. He considers the word positive as a symbol of growth in a larger sense. It is a kind of yoga for him, which means communion with Nature. It is something which elevates, enriches, enlarges, expands and develops him. There is no place here for selfishness, narrowness, mental poverty, parochialism and other constrictions. For him, life is meant for growth in tune with the Nature. He considers himself a part of the whole and sees his survival in the survival of the whole. The difference between giving and receiving ceases to exist for him and he sees it only as a process of natural exchange. Thus, a positive living always means growth-oriented approach, even if it may not appear so explicitly.

So, you see, the power of thinking and discrimination can be our worst enemy, and at the same time, be our best friend. The choice is ours and only we, as human beings, are able to exercise this choice. In this choice lies the greatest significance of human birth. In fact, our whole dignity lies on it. If we choose to be positive, our life becomes meaningful, peaceful, harmonious and fulfilling. Opposite becomes the case when we choose to be negative. A positive thinker is harmonious not only with himself, but also with his environment. His thinking has a positive impact around him and the process perpetuates itself. The same is the case with a negative thinker.

When a larger number of people adopt positive approach, there is greater prosperity and happiness in the society. In the process, the individual is also elevated, coming closer to the true goal of life. Thus, life not only becomes a joy, but also a gateway to further evolution.

It is in this background that Shri Aurobindo talked of superman. If evolution is possible from ape to man, it is certainly possible from man to superman, too. Like the external developments, there are no limits to internal development either. If the process of inner development is continued with sustained effort, it is possible to achieve the state of superconsciousness and become a superman. This is where the importance of human birth lies, provided we understand, accept and practise the laws of positive living. This is not a small agenda. But even a jet starts its journey of thousands miles with a ground speed of zero. Let us also, then, start on the path of positive living by understanding the law of human birth and evolution. This understanding will surely lead us to stress-free living.

Living with a Positive Mindset

I had a cousin who passed away in April 1991 at the age of 58 when he underwent a second bypass surgery in UK. He had a brilliant career in the field of finance and always displayed a positive frame of mind. Despite being quite older than to me, he used to interact with me on various matters and I always enjoyed his company. In a way he was a friend and guide to me in many respects. Incidentally, I was with him in Delhi for some time on the day he left for UK. While parting he gave me a piece of advice saying, "Rakesh, remember one thing—in life, peace at any price is cheap." These were his last words to me and thereafter we had no occasion to meet because he passed away soon after. Obviously these words were the essence of his life which I took with great reverence and emotion. Since then these words keep ringing in my mind and guide me whenever there is possibility of deviation from the path of peace.

Only about a year prior to this incident, I had founded the Kabir Peace Mission with the help of some friends. Its main objective was to develop positive thinking in the society. The advice of my cousin and his subsequent passing away further strengthened my resolve to work in this field and also established the need of it. Today peace eludes most of us despite all our achievements. It is no secret at all that a large number of people today have everything to make an impressive bio-data but do not have peace of mind. The question arises—what is it that goes wrong and what can we do about it ? The main purpose of this discussion is to ponder over this question so that we all get benefited from each other's experiences. It is not the intention to approach the subject from a very philosophical point of view but from a view which is practical and appeals to our common sense.

First of all, we must accept the fact that we are living in an age of scientific and economic development. This development has taken place on account of man's intelligence as well as diligence. Both these faculties are the gifts of Nature to him and therefore any outcome of their deployment in right direction would also be called a natural process. This is exactly what we call the process of Human Evolution. As a result of this process the human race is getting equipped with more and more resources as the time is passing by. I see nothing wrong with this phenomenon and take it in consonance with Nature. The results achieved in the field of science and economics give us not only a great sense of satisfaction but also ample opportunities of outer as well as inner development. If we take such integrated view of progress, it is easy to find an answer to our dilemma.

Second we also have to contemplate over the question of purpose or goal of life. Again one need not be very philosophical in this respect also. A very simple and undisputed answer to this question is that we all want peace and happiness in our lives. The purpose of all our worldly endeavours ultimately is to seek peace and happiness. It is also a fact that no defined parameters of worldly progress are any guarantee to happiness. Thus to say that all rich people are happy will be as wrong as to say that all poor people are unhappy. The same plea can be taken for every parameter of outer progress. Whether it is riches, positions, fame or educational degrees, there is no assured direct relationship between them and happiness. If it is so then certainly we are missing a crucial link between outer progress and happiness. And this takes us to the quality of our mindset which is most crucial to our happiness. Those who have a positive mindset not only achieve outer progress but are happy too. While those with a negative mindset are never happy, no matter how much progress they make externally.

What is a 'Positive Mindset'? Unless we understand it correctly it may be difficult to proceed in this direction. I consider the word 'Positive' to be a symbol of growth in a larger sense. It is no different from the word 'Yoga' which means addition and communion. It is something which elevates, enriches, enlarges, expands and contributes to our growth. It has no place for selfishness, narrowness, mental poverty, parochialism, etc. A person with a positive approach thinks in larger perspective and for greater prosperity. He does not do so as a matter of charity but believes it to be in his interest too. After all, one is a part of the whole and can survive only as long as the whole survives. He gives only to receive, may be in a different form, because he understands that when looked in totality, there is no difference between giving and receiving and it is only a matter of exchange. Thus his approach is always growth oriented and this is what I consider to be a positive mindset. In other words, it is to be in line with Nature. Thus a positive mind is always a part of Nature while the negative one is always apart from Nature. We can also say that being positive is to live effortlessly while being negative needs effort.

This positivity has to be applied to our thinking through the faculty of mind. Our mind is a wonderful gift to us given by Nature but it needs taming through another wonderful faculty called intelligence. Human being is the only creature which is equipped with the capacity to think and discriminate. These two qualities put him at a much higher pedestal vis-à-vis other creatures of Nature. All our outer progress is the result of this power available to us. But there is one thing wrong also with this power. And the wrong is that with such power at our command, we soon start differentiating ourselves from Nature and become the victims. It is like using the same weapon for committing suicide which is given to us for our protection. A negative mind does exactly the same and turns our external progress as a weapon of destroying our happiness. That is why happiness eludes most of us despite all the external prosperity. On the other hand, a positive mind not only helps in achieving greater external progress but also turns it into an opportunity for greater happiness.

A positive mindset makes us true 'Karma-Yogis' and I read a simple test of it in a modern commentary on Gita. The author says that when success is accompanied by peace it is a sure indication of 'Karma-Yoga' and any exception to it needs some correction in our way of working or thinking. He also says that the principle of

Positive Thinking always works provided we are willing to work at it. It is not an easy discipline and needs hard work as well as a strong belief. It also requires honest living and a keen desire to succeed. And we need to keep working at it constantly to achieve success. Just when we believe we have mastered it, we will have to develop it, all again. However, success and peace, can be available to all of us if we understand the true goal of life and live with a positive mindset.

Last, it is helpful to accept the fact that we live in an environment which has a great variety. It is not always necessary to reach a consensus or to give a common answer to all our problems. Perceptions change with person, situation and time. Our perception may be different from others and at times we may not be in a position to act as per our perception. In such a situation, it is wise to accept a different viewpoint if it is in the larger interest to do so. This kind of flexibility is also an indication of a Positive Mindset and brings us more respect than rigidity does.

Be Positive and Motivated at All Times

*L*ife, in general, is a long journey. Like any other journey, we all want to enjoy it but not many succeed. The uncertainty of life makes the process of success even more difficult. Someone has rightly pointed out that half of the life is 'if' (note the middle two alphabets in the word life) and three-fourth is 'lie' (remove 'f' from the word life). Quite often the pattern of life changes greatly with one small incident. It may happen for the better or the worse. If so, does it mean that we all are helpless and have no control on our lives? The answer to this question is in both 'Yes' and 'No'. Yes, in one sense it is true that we really have no control over the events of life. They just happen and we have to accept them as such. I am referring to those events that take place without our being apparently responsible for them. Such events greatly change the pattern of our lives and we often call this phenomenon as 'luck'. The answer is 'No' in the sense that while we have no control over the events, we certainly have control on our responses to them. This is what makes the difference. One person may make his life miserable in a particular set of circumstances and another person may use similar circumstances for achieving the highest objective of life.

Obviously there is a difference between these two persons. One is positive and the other is negative. One is motivated, the other is not. This difference is noticed by all of us and at all times. A positive thinker is always optimistic, cheerful, charming and likable. A negative thinker is always pessimistic, gloomy, repulsive and disliked. As Oscar Wilde has rightly observed: 'There are people who create happiness, wherever they go, others whenever they go'. The other difference is in the level of motivation. One is positively and the other is negatively motivated. In other words, one is motivated and the other is demotivated. In a way both the terms 'Positive Thinking' and 'Motivation' are deeply connected. One cannot exist without the other. They have a chicken-and-egg kind of relationship. It is difficult to say which one comes first. It is, therefore, essential to understand both of them simultaneously. In a general sense it is positive thinking that leads to positive motivation.

Before we proceed further, let us examine the phrase 'Postive Thinking'. The first word of this phrase is 'Positive'. I consider this word to be a symbol of growth in a larger sense. It is not different from the word 'Yoga' which means addition and communion. It is something, which elevates, enriches, enlarges, expands and grows. It has no place for selfishness, narrowness, mental poverty, parochialism and constriction. It is not a matter of charity but essential for our true growth. After all, each one of us is a part of the whole and can survive only as long as the whole survives. One, therefore, gives nothing to others but only to oneself. Thus the process of giving is no different from receiving because, where looked in totality, it is a matter of exchange only. Thus a positive approach always means growth-oriented approach even if it may externally appear otherwise.

The second word 'Thinking' is also equally important. After all, the process of thinking is, what differentiates man from animal. It is a wonderful faculty provided by God to human beings. And it is the quality of thinking, which distinguishes one person from another. Our best friends and our worst enemies are our thoughts. Our dignity depends upon the quality of our thinking. Every action, whether constructive or destructive, begins with a thought. As are the thoughts, so are the actions. Thus our thinking has a great impact on the quality of our actions and in turn on our lives.

With this background it becomes easier to understand the phrase 'Positive Thinking' as something growth-oriented, taking a larger perspective and greater happiness as goal. Here an individual considers himself or herself as a part of the whole and the gain of the whole automatically becomes the gain of the individual. When a larger number of people adopt this approach, there is greater prosperity and happiness in the society. In the process, the individual is also elevated coming closer to the true goal of life. In a way there is no difference between positive thinking and value-based thinking. It may also be called spiritual thinking. When one thinks of spiritual growth, larger growth is automatically implied.

The concept of positive thinking is important in all aspects of life and for all people. It brings both external as well as internal growth. A person may be rich or poor but positive thinking makes his life enriching irrespective of his material possessions. Now, I shall try to relate the concept of positive thinking with professional excellence, the need of which has already been established. We are living in a period, which can easily be called as one of the most challenging one humanity has seen so far. The expectations of a civilised democratic society have grown so much that they pose a great challenge before its managers, be they in any field. In order to meet this challenge, they need to adopt a positive approach. It is my experience that a clear concept of life and its values are of great help in developing a positive approach leading to excellence, contentment, satisfaction and fulfilment in life.

Now, we come to the term 'Motivation'. This word is a derivative of the word 'Motive', the dictionary meaning of which is concerned with the initiation of action. It is a symbol of human dynamism. As long as we are alive, we cannot escape action. What action we do, depends upon our motivation. Thus motivation plays a very important role in the shaping of our lives. If we are positively motivated, our life becomes not only pleasant but also a source of inspiration for others, thus motivating them too. In fact, motivation is something which comes from within. No one can motivate others, one can only inspire them to motivate themselves. Motivation, which comes from within, is long lasting too. Motivation is a willing urge to do a thing without being forced by anyone. It makes us a willing worker and increases our satisfaction. It reduces our stress and makes us feel happy and successful.

Motivation is of two kinds. It can either be external or internal. Again, external motivation has two kinds, namely fear motivation and incentive motivation. Fear motivation is short-lived and goes away with the motivating factor. Even fear is overcome after some time. While incentive motivation is better than fear motivation, it is also temporary. Its intensity comes down with time and greater incentive is required to maintain the same level of motivation. After some time the incentive is also taken for granted. It is only the internal or self-motivation, which stays with time, gives maximum satisfaction and needs no supervision. Only when the motivation is self-generated, it can stay for long.

Here it will also be useful to understand that it is not essential that the same factors motivate all of us. Studies show that different people are motivated by different factors. One factor, which may motivate someone, may not do so to the other. However, the basic factors are the same. We all want to perform well, to be appreciated and to be successful. Any step taken to fulfil these basic instincts is a help in self-motivating process. A sincere word of appreciation can do wonders. Also the same person can have different kinds of motivation in different circumstances. The greatest motivation comes from a person's belief system. That means he needs to believe in what he does and accepts responsibility. When people accept responsibility for their behaviour and action, their attitude towards life becomes positive. They become more productive personally and professionally. Their relationships improve both at home and at work. Life then also becomes more meaningful and fulfilled.

After a person's basic physical needs are met, emotional needs become a bigger motivator. We must understand that every behaviour comes out of the 'pain or gain' principle. If the gain is greater than the pain, that is the motivation. If the pain is greater than the gain, then that is a deterrent. Gain can be tangible, such as: monetary rewards, vacations, and gifts. They can be intangible, such as: recognition, appreciation, sense of achievement, promotion, growth, responsibility, accomplishment, etc. Experience has shown that people do a lot for money, more for a good leader and most for a belief. People die for a belief. If somehow the belief system can be changed for the better, motivation will follow on its own. When we believe that we are responsible for our lives and our behaviour, our outlook towards life changes for the better.

Thus 'Positive Thinking' and 'Motivation' are directly connected with our attitude towards life. If our attitude is larger and we see ourselves as a part of the whole, we are likely to remain positive and motivated. Greater is the expansion in our thinking, greater are the chances of permanence in our positivity and motivation. Naturally, it cannot come in a day. One has to strive for it. There are no shortcuts. If someone suggests a shortcut, it will be equally short-lived too. But the principles of positive thinking and motivation always work, provided, we are willing to work at them. It is not an easy discipline. It takes hard work and strong belief. It also requires honest living and a keen desire to succeed. And we will need to keep working at it constantly to achieve success. Just when we believe we have mastered it, we will have to develop it again. At times, there will be frustration but we must remember the following poem:

People are unreasonable, illogical and self-centred.

Love them anyway.

If you do good, people will accuse you of selfish ulterior motives.

Do good anyway.

If you are successful, you win false friends and true enemies.

Succeed anyway.

The good you do today will be forgotten tomorrow.

Do good anyway.

People favour underdogs but follow only topdogs.

Fight for some underdogs anyway.

What you spend years building may be destroyed overnight.

Build anyway.

People really need help but may attack you if you help them.

Help people anyway.

Give the world the best you have and you'll get kicked in the teeth.

Give the world the best you've got anyway.

Thus a positive thinker always remains motivated irrespective of what he gets from the outer world. He is very clear and convinced in his approach and success is always available to him. Such persons change things for the better not only for themselves but for others too.